T0212326

Technological and Business Fundamentals for Mobile App Development

Tamie Salter

Technological and Business Fundamentals for Mobile App Development

 Springer

Tamie Salter
Citizen Alert Inc.
Sherbrooke, QC, Canada

Logos and other graphic elements are meant for educational and accessibility purposes only

ISBN 978-3-031-13854-6   ISBN 978-3-031-13855-3   (eBook)
https://doi.org/10.1007/978-3-031-13855-3

This Springer imprint is published by the registered company Springer Nature Switzerland AG
The registered company address is: Gewerbestrasse 11, 6330 Cham, Switzerland

This book is dedicated to my son Vincent Salter and all the people (family, friends, colleagues, and strangers) that have helped me throughout my personal and professional life. They are far too numerous to mention in person. Without these people's kindness I would not be in a position to write this book. It is hard for me to imagine that at the age of 26 I had no formal education, and I was living in homeless accommodation as a single mother to a young baby, my son Vincent.

This book is most graciously dedicated to everyone that helped me on the journey of pursuing an education all the way to obtaining my PhD in robotics, through my failures and successes at business, but more importantly to those who helped me on the long road and through journey to a happy life.

I hope that my story will give inspiration to anyone that feels lost in life. I also hope that people will take the information in this book and use it to develop amazing apps that benefit mankind in some small or large way or to perhaps just simply to help anyone in need. As I finish writing this book war is raging in Ukraine and the world is facing many different climate disasters. Wouldn't it be wonderful if there were simple apps to help with things such as the handling of the logistics of a large influx of refugees or perhaps to help those facing the challenges of losing their home due to fire or flood.

My hope is that some amazing app will spring from the information provided within the pages.

About This Book

This textbook has been written to help anyone that is embarking on the journey of learning to create an app for mobile devices. People that begin developing apps often come from a specific background such as computer science or business. The skills required to fully understand what makes a great app span many different domains. You will need to understand lots of different concepts regardless of your main area of expertise or domain of choice. There are many reasons a person could be thinking about developing an app. Whatever your reason, *perhaps you are in business and want an app for your company or you just had a really good idea for an app and want to develop it, or perhaps you are studying computer science and want to make a brilliant new game,* you will need a broad spectrum of knowledge. There are many topics that you must have a fundamental understanding of when beginning the process of developing an app, so that the app will be well thought out and successful. In this book, we will walk you through the steps of creating a successful app whatever your reason for developing one.

Examples of why you need this book are that computer science students will not be taught about 'target markets' during their computer science degree. Nor will business students be taught a fundamental understanding of how to code an app so that it is future friendly and will cut down on the amount it needs to be updated via the app stores. This is why this book has been written to give the fundamental knowledge required by everyone regardless of their background or their role in app development.

Teaching tools used in this book are written chapters, graphical images, and links to online videos in addition to work exercises to help you put into practice the concepts being taught.

The aim of this book is to give you an overview of the different elements that are needed to develop a successful app. In this book, we will go over techniques, tips, and resources that will come in handy if you are planning to create a mobile device app.

Topics are separated into chapters so that you can go over the topics one at a time and develop a strong foundation in that particular topic before moving on to the next.

Whether you are a programmer, a student, a business person, or a musician, this book will be useful for you. Whatever your background, if you want to be in app development, you will need to have a general understanding about *all* the topics taught in this book. This book will provide knowledge that is:

1. ***Technical*** – covering topics like programming, types of apps, and various technologies.
2. ***Non-technical*** – covering topics like design, marketing the app, revenue, and budgets.

Each chapter in the book will clearly set a topic and goal for the chapter. Some chapters will have exercises for you to complete to increase your understanding of the topic. There will also be links to videos and articles to help your understanding.

The chapters are organized as follows:

Chapter 1: Necessary Skills and Steps
Chapter 2: Key Ingredients
Chapter 3: Design/UI/UX
Chapter 4: Technology & Technical Development
Chapter 5: Security/Compliance/Getting Accepted
Chapter 6: Monetization
Chapter 7: Budget/Project Management/Marketing

Notice

You are receiving this book in its first version of the 2022 edition. The topic of this book is extremely fluid and changes frequently. Please make sure you have the latest edition to have the most up to date information. If you are using an older version than the current year, please make sure to research each of the topics to see how they have changed after the publication of this book. For further information, you may email the author at: textbook@tamie.org. Professors may email the author for further teacher resources.

Thank you

Disclaimer

The Technological and Business Fundamentals for Mobile App Development is an independent (publication) and has not been authorized, sponsored, or otherwise approved by any of the companies mentioned in this book.

Contents

Overview of Steps and Necessary Skills

1

In this first chapter, we'll focus on the project as a whole, looking at how to break it down into various topics and then at how to move through the necessary phases of development to get to the final product: a successful app.

Goal of This Chapter

This chapter will help you understand how to break your complete app development project up into steps. Each step will be clearly defined and will include the process you need to go through to complete that step.

Vocabulary Introduced

We introduce the following vocabulary:

- Skills
  - The various skills that must be combined to create an app.
- Steps
  - The process of carrying out a series of systematic steps to create an app.
- Core understanding
  - Despite your background (computer science/business/creative) you should have a core understanding of these topics
- Technical understanding
  - A deeper understanding of topics listed as technical is required for those that choose to purse a technical path such as computer science.
- Non-Technical understanding
  - A deeper understanding of topics listed as non-technical is required for those that choose to purse a non-technical path such as business or creative.
- Component/Features of an app

T. Salter, *Technological and Business Fundamentals for Mobile App Development*, https://doi.org/10.1007/978-3-031-13855-3_1

- The components or features of an app that form the base of the app's functionality.
- Evaluating apps
  - Being able to evaluate an app's components, features, design, functionality.
- Analyzing apps
  - Begin able to analyze an app's components, features, design, functionality to see if it is suitable for its target market.

Levels of Understanding

Below in Fig. 1.1 we see a breakdown of knowledge required for app development broken into overall categories.

These categories will enable you to be able to effectively look at an app development project from a holistic view point.

- We see the core knowledge required which covers topics such as Skill requirements, how to be able to know the components/features of an app, plus how to be able evaluate and analyse not only your own app but other people's as well.
- Expanded Non-Technical in this area requires a deeper understanding of effectively evaluating and analysing an apps features, components and functionality for its target market.
- Expanded Technical knowledge required including a deeper understanding of topics such as; what is required technically to achieve the requested features, components and functionality?

Content

From Ideation to Implementation: Steps to a Successful App

To develop a successful app, it is important to outline the steps needed to reach the final product. Whether you are a new tech start-up, working by yourself in a garage,

Fig. 1.1   Core, non-technical and technical for this chapter

or working for an app development company, certain steps must be followed throughout the app development process. The Business of Apps [1] tells us that there are four stages to app development, listing these stages as; Pre-Design, Design, Development and Support. You can other suggestions that include five phases, six phases and so on. The steps/phases presented have come from the author's experience of developing apps for over 10 years. The author has overseen the development of various types of apps, from apps that control robots to apps that are free of charge aimed at the general public, to apps aimed at businesses that are paid for apps. The author's experience also comes from having spent time in both academia teaching app development and commercial business where the sole income for the company was the sale of apps.

To create a great app, it is important to follow a series of steps. Below is a list of steps to follow. You do not have to follow this exact list but you must go through a process and a series of steps to create a well thought out app. A great app will not come from just jumping in and coding and then releasing the outcome to the app stores. Not having a fundamental understanding of all the topics that go into app development plus not following a systematic series of steps will result in an inferior app. This book recommends the steps below, feel free to add or subtract from this list. If you do deviate from this list make sure you understand why you can skip a step or why you need to add a step. This knowledge will come with time as you become more competent at the different steps.

You may have had a brilliant idea for a new app or you may have been given the task to develop an app by someone else. You need to know how to break the app idea as a whole into various categories or domains to help you create the best app possible. You need to be able to recognize the different domains that must all come together to make an app. In this first step, begin thinking about the app in terms of each of the following domains:

- Concept Design/UI/UX
- Key ingredients
- Technical development
- Testing
- Compliance
- Market
- Budget
- Business model
- Revenue/Monetization

The steps are listed here for use once you have completed the book and understand how they will apply to your project.

Steps to Complete

Step 1: The beginning
- You have an idea for an app or you are given an idea for an app to develop. Great! This is the beginning of the development process. Take some time to write down the idea and begin to map it out as a whole. Step one is covered in detail in this chapter. Something to ask yourself during this process is ... 'do you have the skills required to develop this app'? Later in this chapter you will find a skills checklist to help you determine this. Do I have the tools necessary to develop the app? If you don't have either the skills or the tools, how will you get them? Equipment and project management will be covered in more detail in Chap. 7: Budget/Project Management/Research/Marketing.

Step 2: Key ingredients
- List the features you want to include in the app, take time to get to know the end user, use the four Ws, learn how to evaluate current apps and how to evaluate whether your ideas will make for a successful app. This step is covered in detail in Chap. 2: Key Ingredients for a Great App.

Step 3: Concept Design/UI/UX/mock-up
- Now it is time to design, to begin working out your user interface and your user experience. This will include making a mock-up of your app. This step will be covered in Chap. 3: *Concept Design*. Once you have completed a first version design User Testing is vitally important. In this step, you will ask potential users to test your app and provide you with feedback. This is the research and analysis phase of your app development. begin testing this product on users, to see how they like it, if they can use it, and if it works the way it is supposed to work. Show your testers your mock-up and see if they like your app. This step will be covered in Chap. 3: *Concept Design*

Step 4: Technology and development
- Make a decision about the right type of app to develop. Learn about the different types of apps and what type will best suit your app. Once you have decided which type of app you want, you will need to decide how to develop it, what programming language should be used, and what development environment will you use. This step is covered in Chap. 4: Technology & Technical Development.

Step 5: Compliance and trends
- Learn about compliance and how to make sure that you can get your app on the app stores (Google Play and Apple). This step is covered in Chap. 5: Trends/Digital Security/Compliance/Getting Accepted.

Step 6: Iterate
- Repeat steps 1 to 5 until you are happy with your product.

Step 7: App economics
- Learn how to monetize your app. There are various ways to make money from apps, and we will investigate them in Chap. 6: *Monetization*.

Step 8: Project management, marketing and submission

- In Step 8, you will be ready to upload your well-designed, well-thought-out with potential app to the app stores. Now you must begin marketing your app to get it known. What digital techniques are there to help you market your app? This step will be covered in Chap. 7: Budget/Project Management/ Research/Marketing.

Skills Requirements

How do you fit into the app development process? Remember that there are many different domains within app development as a whole. App development encompasses a wide range of disciplines, including a variety of roles that are technical, non-technical, and some that are crossover and require both technical and non-technical knowledge. What do you want to be? What are your aspirations? Whatever domain you hope to excel in, you must have knowledge of all of the topics in this book. You cannot program a brilliant app if you have no understanding of end-user requirements. And you cannot graphically design an amazing app if you have no understanding of what it takes to program your design. As a business person, you can have a fantastic idea of a lucrative app, but if you do not understand what it takes to get bring idea to life, then you likely won't make any money at all!

Whatever domain within app development you focus on or come from you, remember to take the time to go over each chapter of this book so that you will better understand the entire app development process. Once you have that knowledge, you will be ready to produce that new, ground breaking app!

Let's begin by examining the different skills required to make an app.

Look at the skills checklist below and consider what your strengths are, what kinds of things you enjoy doing, and what direction you think you would like to go within the many domains of app development.

Skills Checklist
Technical components

- Coding/Programming
  - Languages
  - Architecture
  - Development environments
  - Native IDEs
  - Hybrid IDEs
  - Web technologies
- Types of Apps
  - Native
  - Hybrid
  - Progressive
- Technologies
  - Servers/The cloud

- Data in motion
- Data at rest
- Digital security
- Personal data security
- Network infrastructure
- Hardware technology, e.g. Bluetooth, accelerometer
- Future technology trends

Non-technical components
- Artistic
  - Digital design programs
  - UI/UX
  - Concept Design
  - Look and feel
  - Graphics
  - Branding
- End-user trials
- Budgets
- Business
- Project Management
- App stores
  - Compliance
  - Uploading
  - Marketing material
- Marketing
  - Digital marketing
  - Communications
  - Mass emailing
  - Press releases
  - Advertising
- User testing
- Research and development
- Questionnaires
- Iterations
- Development methodologies
- Overall decisions
- Budgets

You should think about the current skills you have, the ones you want to develop, and the ones that you will need to be involved in app development.

- Which skills do you want to improve on?
- If you a tech person, you will still need an understanding of some business/marketing skills

- If you are a business or non-tech person, you will still need an understanding of what programming is, what are the current technologies, which direction technology is going in, etc.

Chapter Summary

In this first chapter, we showed you how to think of the project as a whole. How to use steps to break it down into various topics and then at how to move through the necessary phases of development to get to the final product: a successful app.

Exercises

Below is an of exercise to help increase your understanding of the terminology, concepts and material presented in this Chapter: Overview of Steps and Necessary Skills

Exercise No 1

The beginning idea is

....
....
....
....
....
....

My Skills are:

....
....
....
....
....
....

I cannot do/have no interest in:

....
....
....
....
....
....

I need to find:

....
....

....

....

....

....

Individual Reflection

To solidify your understanding in 200 words write out what you have learnt from this chapter. Here are some hints that you might use to write about.

- What you have learned about the different skills that need to be combined to make an app
- Write about what are the steps that are needed to be completed to make a well thought out app
- Do you consider yourself to be technical or non-technical?

Knowledge Check

Fill in the blanks of the following sentence:
 Use the words provided in the word bank.
 Every app project consists of areas that require ....
 plus .... *and* .... *to be known by every-one on the team whether you are technical or non-technical person. To complete any app project you must follow a series of* ....
 Word Bank:
 Core Knowledge, Technical Knowledge, Non-Technical Knowledge, Steps.

Answers

Below are suggested answers to the exercise given in this chapter. They are not complete and simply a suggestion to help you further think about your own solutions. You may well come up with a different or better solution. This is part of the app development process.

Exercise No. 1

•The beginning idea is
What is your basic idea?
Examples
  A recipe app – an easy to use recipe app for people wanting recipe based on various selection types such as, cultural food, vegetarian.
  A word puzzle app – a complex guess the word within 10 attempts. With a leader board showing users achievements.
  A insurance app – a way to easily report claims and keep track of the claim process.
•My Skills are:
Examples
  Coding – I am able to code in web technologies
  Coding – I am proficient in native technologies
  Designer – I am a graphic designer and I am very interested in being an entrepreneur
•I cannot do/have no interest in:
Examples
  Programming.
  Design/Graphics
  Marketing
•I need to find:
Examples
  A person that I can pay hourly to code my app
  A partner who technical
  A partner who understands business
  A person that I can pay hourly to produce the graphics

Knowledge Check Answer

*Every app project consists of areas that require **core knowledge** plus **technical knowledge** and **non-technical knowledge** to be known by everyone on the team whether you are technical or non-technical person. To complete any app project you must follow a series of **steps**.*

Key Ingredients for a Great App

2

All apps require certain key elements to make it a successful, engaging, useful, used, wanted and downloaded app. In this book we call these elements 'Key Ingredients'. Whilst a single app may not need all of the key ingredients, each of these ingredients is vital in general app development and you need to know, and understand them, to develop a successful app. This knowledge spans both technical and non-technical app development. So, whether you are a Startup CEO or a computer programmer use these key ingredients. When implemented and combined together, these ingredients will result in a successful app.

Goal of This Chapter

The goal of this chapter is to teach you about the essential ingredients required for any app. After reading this chapter you should be able to analyze your own project and be able to ascertain if your app has the key ingredients it requires to make a great app. If not, you will have the knowledge to change your app to make sure it includes the 'Key Ingredient' it may be missing.

Vocabulary Introduced

- Key Ingredients
  - The features, functionality and things that must be considered for every app.
- The Four Ws
  - Using the Four Ws will help you to get to know your end user
- Designed
  - This term can be applied to multiple area. Generally this means that every area of an app should be well thought out.

- Features of an app
  - During the design process these are the core functionality of an app that can be broken down into 'nice to have' or 'necessary'.
- Valuable
  - To be useful apps must provide some value. Value could come in a never amount of scenarios such as, entertainment, translation, tracking health. You must decide on what value the app will provide to the end user.
- Discoverability
  - This is the process of how an end user will discover your app. It is easy or hard for them to discover?
- Accessibility/Inclusivity
  - This is the process of making sure that your app can be used by everyone.
- Localized
  - Adapting your app to meet various localizations such as, languages, cultural norms.
- Forward Thinking
  - The process of thinking about the possible future in everything from technology trends, various new functionality to end user trends.
- Delightful
  - Making it a pleasure to use an app. The app easily and effectively achieves it goals whether they are entertainment or utility
- Innovative
  - Innovation often involves making something easier for your end user. It is what sets apps apart.

Levels of Understanding

Below in Fig. 2.1 we see a breakdown of knowledge required to be able to effectively look at the features and key ingredients of any app.

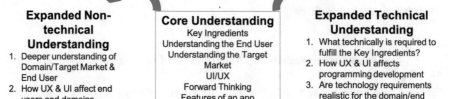

Expanded Non-technical Understanding
1. Deeper understanding of Domain/Target Market & End User
2. How UX & UI affect end users and domains
3. Possible user requirements in the future
4. Expanded understanding of an accessibility needs
5. Localisation: which markets is the app likely to used in?

Core Understanding
Key Ingredients
Understanding the End User
Understanding the Target Market
UI/UX
Forward Thinking
Features of an app

Expanded Technical Understanding
1. What technically is required to fulfill the Key Ingredients?
2. How UX & UI affects programming development
3. Are technology requirements realistic for the domain/end user?
4. How to program for accessibility and localisation

Fig. 2.1   Core, non-technical and technical for this chapter

- We see the core knowledge required which covers topics such as Key Ingredients that all apps should have.
- Expanded Non-Technical in this area requires a deeper understanding of target markets and end users.
- Expanded Technical knowledge required including a deeper understanding of topics such as what technology is required to fulfil the Key Ingredients of the app

Content

Introduction

Developing an app is a very exciting experience and you might just want to dive straight in and get going on your project. However, you should take some time to plan a little before beginning. A great place to start is learning and understanding the key ingredients to what makes a great app. If you know the key ingredients needed for an app, you can quickly begin to plan out the app you are developing. Implementing these key ingredients will help you develop a great app. In this chapter we will go over the ten key ingredients you need to know.

In this chapter, we will break the key ingredients up for you into different topics and teach you the knowledge you need to build them into your app. We will look at each of the ten key ingredients one by one, clearly explaining to you why you need to implement them. By looking at each of the ten key ingredients individually, you will develop a good foundational knowledge for each topic.

People may have different ideas about what makes a great app. People may have different key ingredients and, certainly, key ingredients will change over time. New technologies will come about, new devices will come out, ways of interacting with technology will change, and the key ingredients required to make a great app will change.

At this moment in time, however, we believe these are the key ingredients that are required to develop a successful app.

In this book, we have talked about making an app a success but success can be defined in many different ways. In terms of an app, what would success look like to you?

- Making a lot of money
- Helping people easily deposit a cheque in their bank account
- Helping people lose weight
- Helping people to easily communicate with the residents in their town
- Teaching children to read

What would make your app successful to you? Whatever your reason for making an app, the following list of key ingredients will help make it a success:

1. The Four Ws
2. Designed
3. Valuable
4. Discoverability
5. Forward Thinking
6. Accessibility/Inclusivity
7. Localized
8. Features

Key Ingredient No. 1: The Four Ws

The Four Ws consist of:

1. Who
2. Why
3. Where
4. When

You must know these four fundamentals about your end user. The app is for the end user – not you. You must understand the end user and how they want the app to be, how they will use it, why they will use it, and so on.

It is possible to broadly term the Four Ws as the target market:

Which domain/target market:

- What is the app going to be used for?
- How does the domain affect the app?
- Do you need to make special concessions because of the domain?
- What are users expecting from an app aimed at this domain?
- Is there a need for this app?

Always know the following about your end user(s):

- (1) Who is using your app.
- (2) Why they are using it.
- (3) Where they are using it.
- (4) When they are using it.

Some of these categories may overlap. For instance, your user may be using your app because they need a language translated (why – translation/foreign country) and they are using it in a foreign country (where – foreign country). But the where needs to be considered as much as the why because maybe they do not have a foreign data plan for the device they are using at a foreign train station.

We shall now look more closely at the individual Four Ws.

WHO

Profile your end user. Get to know them. Think about what they may be like, about the things that make them distinctive.

Who is the typical end user of your app?

Maybe the app is a bedtime story-telling app. Will the end user be the *child/children* or the *parent(s)/Adult(s)*?

Do you need to consider both the parents and the children in your planning? Apple produces lots of good videos about considering things such as the end user. They have a video on giving insights into developing an app aimed at children's learning. At the time of printing Apple's videos on various topics can be found here:

- https://developer.apple.com/videos/

Are there features that must be adjusted to suit your end user's needs?

- Gender (Male/Female/Non-binary/Any)
- Age (Child/Young adult/Adult/Senior)
- Location (Italy/Europe/America/China)
- Likes/dislikes? Colours, sounds, flashing images?
- Disabilities? Dyslexia, motor skills, vision issues?
- Tech savvy? Do they want the latest tech, do they hate it when their interface changes?

Always know your end user and test on your end user, check that your assumptions are correct.

It is important to understand your end user and discover who they are. Is your app a fitness app aimed at senior citizens? If so, it should be designed differently than it would be for athletes or for children with type two diabetes.

Think about the technology your end user is using. Will it work for the app?

If you are making a fitness app for senior citizens and you use voice recognition, can it correctly understand a person when they are panting? Does the senior citizen have a device with a microphone in it? Can a senior citizen master swiping right with their thumb? Can a child swipe right with their fingers?

WHY

Why is your end user using your app? What is your end user trying to achieve by using your app?

Functionality?
- Are they doing something they find challenging?
- Are they doing something that they do all the time?
- Are they using your app for something that they have done on other similar apps? If this is the case, do you need to follow other apps with a familiar feel or do you need to find a new, innovative way to achieve your end user's goals

Fun?
- Is the app pure entertainment?
- Is it an educational game?
- Is it for a child or adult?
- Is it a joke app or is it a serious gaming league?

Work?
- Does the app belong to a company?
- Is the user an employee?
- Who has the final say in the length of time to complete a task?
- Does the company want a lot of information input? Maybe a weekly schedule that the employee has achieved?

Utility?
- Is the user trying to order a hamburger?
- Does this need to be quick or engaging?
- Will a user keep a utility app on their phone?
- Do you need to consider how large the file size is for apps that are for utility purposes?

WHERE
Where are the end users using your app?

- In the dark
- In class
- In a different country
- At home
- Wi-Fi/Network capabilities
- Cell phone/mobile signal capabilities
- While driving
- On the subway/underground

WHEN
When are the end users using your app?

- While jogging
- While driving
- In the early morning
- While in danger

Is there anything distinctive about where or when your end user is using your app?

Key Ingredient No. 2: Designed

You cannot escape design in app development. It is so important that the whole next chapter (Chapter 3: *Concept Design*) is devoted to just this subject. Here, we will briefly say that whether you intend to be a back end developer (see Glossary), a business person, or whether you work within any domain in the app development world, you must know about design.

Key Ingredient No. 3: Valuable

Often a business/marketing person will ask you… What is the value proposition for your app? What does the term *value proposition* mean?

A value proposition explains how your product:

- Solves your customers' problems or improves their situation (**relevancy**)
- Provides a specific benefit (**quantified value**)
- Makes your app unique and different from other apps (**unique differentiation**)

Thinking about your value proposition will help you to decide on monetization strategy (see Chap. 6: *Monetization*).

Your app must provide some sort of value to your end user. This could come in many different forms:

- Goals
- Fun
- Learning

Help the end user achieve a goal:

- Losing weight
- Teaching their children to read
- Teaching the end user a new language
- Entertaining the end user
- Waking a hard to wake student up
- Getting a student to class on time
- Help the end user have fun
- A crossword
- A word puzzle
- Watching cat videos
- Playing a high octane game
- Seeing pictures of a grandchild
- How to draw (could you do this on a small screen?)

Perhaps value to your end user is socializing, perhaps it is swiping right on a picture. Finding love is always deemed very valuable to people. Perhaps it is the fact that they don't need to go to the library to get a book. There are endless ways mobile apps can be of value.

You must check that what you are developing has value to some people/end users. This will become even more important if you want to make money from your app or if you want to charge for it. If there is no perceived value by the end user, they will not be prepared to pay for:

- Coins in a game
- The cost of a newspaper app

Reflection Questions:
- Think of some apps that you have
- Think of the value the give to you

How can you know if an app will provide value?
A good place to start is by thinking of:

- A need
- An issue
- A desire
- A problem
- A want

Does your app solve any of these points for your end user?

Key Ingredient No. 4: Discoverability
Discoverability is a very important topic. How will people find your app? Through an app store? How are you going to be sure that people see your app in app store search results? Will they find it because of your name? Is your name going to be a brand? Like Google? Or are you going to use a name that easily signifies what your app does, such as "My To-Do List"? Are you developing an app for a customer, maybe a bank, and you will be given details, such as the name, the text, etc. Do you know how many characters you can fit under an icon on a home screen? Maybe the name you are thinking of will need to be shortened.

When thinking about how people will find an app that you are developing…

Think about your own behaviour. Do you search the web first or do you just go straight to an app store? How many different screens do you scroll through to find the app you are looking for? When a user searches on an app store, the owner of that app store will use different forms of metadata from your app to decide whether to show your app or not in the search results.

How, exactly, the app store owner (company) decides which apps to display will be proprietary information, but there are somethings that we can quite accurately guess at:

- Your app's name (title)
- The store information you filled in, including things like keywords. If your app store information includes 'To-do list' often, you can imagine that you may be shown if someone searches for that term
- Which category you chose for your app
- Number of downloads
- Ratings and reviews

Users must be able to find your app to use it. It is your job to make sure they can. Otherwise all your hard work will have gone to waste. You should build discoverability into your initial design. Tips to make your app discoverable:

- Pick names that signify what your app does
- Think about app store character limits when naming your app
- Have an icon that resembles what your app does

If you have a huge marketing budget, you can be more flexible in your decisions.

Key Ingredient No. 5: Forward Thinking
Will the app you are developing still be relevant in 6 months? Will the app be functioning in 6 months? As an app developer, you must always think towards the future. The app world changes extremely quickly and you must be able to keep up.

To keep your app relevant, think about the future for:

- Apps in general
- Design and UI/UX

Consider:

- Does the future need to be thought about in the code?
- How do you code for the future?

Also consider practical details, such as:

- How will the app be maintained?
- What will you do if you need to update the design of the app?

Apps are cutting-edge technology. The domain you are choosing to enter is one of the future. It is fast-paced and it changes rapidly. You must always be thinking about the future when developing an app.

This can be broken down into different categories.

- Design
- Code
- Technology

- Security
- Trends
- Compliance issues

Design (see more in Chap. 3: *Concept Design*)

- Can I adapt the design of the UI/UX if design trends change?
- What are future design trends? How will I keep abreast of them?

Coding Technology (see more in Chap. 4: Technology & Technical Development)

- How will we choose to code the app?
- What programming language and environment will give me the best chance of staying up-to-date with technological challenges?
- Can you code this app in a way that will ensure that in the future you can easily add or adjust features of the app?

Hardware technology (see more in Chap. 4: Technology & Technical Development).

- What happens if a new device or screen size comes out?
- How will you support the latest OS releases?
- How will you integrate the latest technologies?
- How will you use the latest development techniques?
- Will it be fast and responsive?

Key Ingredient No. 6: Accessibility/Inclusivity
Accessibility or inclusivity is a term used to encompass the idea that the software/app you plan to develop will be made accessible to all people, including those who have some form of disability or challenge. In other words, accessibility/inclusivity ensures your app is accessible to all people.

- Have you ever thought about how people with challenges use apps?
- What about people with vision issues/reading issues?
- What about people with dexterity issues?
- What is the percentage of your target market that may have accessibility issues?

In Apple products such as adding a colour tint to the screen can be found under the accessibility system setting. This function is useful for anyone who wants to use a device at night but doesn't want light interference to affect their sleep. Therefore an accessibility feature can be useful to everyone.

When you plan and design your app, always consider accessibility or, as some might say, design it for everyone (inclusivity). If you design for accessibility, you know that everyone will be able to use your app. Think about the differently abled: the hearing, vision, motion, or learning impaired. Accessibility can also be thought of as Inclusivity. Apple tells us to design for inclusivity. In Table 2.1, we see the different ways we can break up the diversity we can find in all people. In this video Apple tells us that designing for inclusivity will "Empower and delight everyone".

Apple has many videos on inclusivity that can be found at:

- developer.apple.com

Below in Table 2.1: Diversity axes we see a table that gives a graphical representation and very brief description of the different axes that you can consider when designing your app. This is an extensive list. You may not need to consider all of the diversity axes but you should consider as many as possible.

Accessibility is now a legal obligation in many countries, such as within the EU and also in smaller jurisdictions such as Ontario, Canada. If you design with

Table 2.1 Diversity axes

Class		Social economic status
Culture		Different world cultures/local cultures
Ethnicity		Different ethnicities
Language		Different languages/langue abilities
Education		Level of education
Political beliefs		Political beliefs
Philosophical beliefs		Philosophical belief
Religion		Various regions and practices
Gender		Gender/Non Gender
Age		Age group
Abilities/disabilities		Abilities or different abilities/disabilities
Handedness		Left/right handed
Body measurements		Different sizes etc
Environment		Type of environment (multitude of variations)
Location		Geo location
Connectivity		Connectivity capabilities
Modern tech		What type of tech

accessibility in mind, you will increase your market share and not be caught out by legal obligations.

Apple offers a variety of video on their developer website. For a general understanding on the topic of accessibility and inclusivity plus to learn how easy it is to code for inclusivity go to: developer.apple.com and use the resources they provide free of charge.

This book was written using the font Arial. This follows guidelines from the following paper on which fonts are easiest for those with dyslexia to read.

- http://dyslexiahelp.umich.edu/sites/default/files/good_fonts_for_dyslexia_ study.pdf

Key Ingredient No. 7: Localization

As developers, we want our apps to be used by as many people as possible. A way to achieve this is by localizing the app. What is localisation?

App Localization means making sure your app functions in different countries, for people of different cultures, and for people who speak different languages.

Is it just about adding multiple languages? No, there is more to localisation than that. Localisation can encompass language, spelling, design, colouring, cultural considerations, and more. Things that can be localized include calendars and time zones; It is even possible to localize things like colours and photographs to better suit your market.

Localizing an app will also make it more delightful for the user to use. Even if you do not localize your app at the very beginning, build the idea into the app from the start and then it will be easy to add localization elements in the future.

Generally, localisation can be broken down into two categories:

- The concept design of the app
- The code behind the app

When you begin the planning/design phase, consider things such as:

- What languages/time zones will you need to think about?
- Think of how many more potential users you can have by simply adding one extra language, such as Spanish, to your app. At the time of publication, there are 379 million native English speakers versus 480 million native Spanish speakers in the world. (2)

Do you see now how a little bit of localization can greatly increase the number of users you will have? Imagine if your first language is not English, but every app you use is in English. And then there is one app in Spanish, your native language, which one would you use most often?

However, languages offer their challenges. When you are designing the app you must consider things like words on the screen:

- Are they longer in different languages?
- How would this affect the interface of the app?

Fig. 2.2 Showing a
localized app

We shall look at various design aspects of localization in an app in the design chapter of this book.

The best way localize the code is to build localization into the code from the very beginning. This means that we must develop the code architecture in such a way that localization is built into it from the start, even if you don't use it straight away. It does not take a great deal of effort to make the code base of an app localized (Fig. 2.2).

Key Ingredient No. 8: Features

A key ingredient to any app is its main features. Being able to understand what are the features of an app that make it useful or entertaining is an important concept. Being able to break an app up into its key features is essential. You must learn to be able to decipher what the key features of the app are. This normally begins with the question: what must the app do? This task comes before any design elements are added. Once you have your list of features, you can begin designing.

What is a 'feature' of an app? A 'feature' can be thought of as an attribute or characteristic of something. So the features of an app are the attributes or characteristics that make that app unique such as, functionality or purpose of the app. As you progress through the app development process you will get more and more refined features.

Begin by making a list of necessary vs. nice-to-have features. Remember to Keep It Simple Stupid – KISS. Start with only the necessary features, design elements, buttons, navigation, etc. You can always add other features at a later time.

The list of features will be different for every app. They can even change from one type of app to another (or even in different versions of a similar app, such as one kind of *to-do-list* when compared to a different *to-do-list* app). You must think about what the app is trying to achieve. Is the app attempting to be the most sophisticated feature filled *to-do-list* app in the world or is the app attempting to be a simple, easy-to-use, free-of-charge *to-do-list*. As the developer/designer, you will need to decide.

To recap what we have learnt: design is extremely important. It can make or break an app.

1. Think *simple* to begin with
2. Think *function* over *design*
3. What are the four *W's*? See: Key Ingredient No. 1: The Four Ws
4. Make a list of *features* (needed, nice-to-have) See: Key Ingredient No. 8: Features
5. *Iterate, iterate, iterate, and learn!*

Chapter Summary

This chapter aimed to teach you that there are some essential ingredients required for any app to achieve the goal of being useful. We aimed to help you learn how to analyze apps including your own project to see if the app(s) have these ingredients (Fig. 2.3).

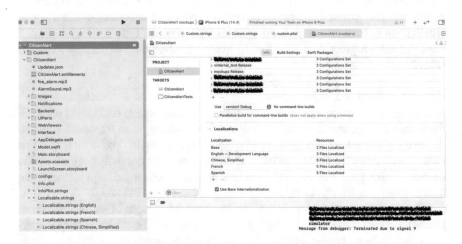

Fig. 2.3 Showing the localization screen of a software project

Fig. 2.4 Showing a dashboard

Case Study: Design/Sound

Citizen Alert Inc. sends out alerts to the citizens of towns. The app offers town administrators a dashboard from which they can send alerts to the population.

Think about when your user will be using your app. If they are jogging, do you need to adjust the user interface? Do you analyze accelerometer and GPS data to decide when the user is jogging? Or do allow the user to tap a start button and then adjust the user interface? Or do you just make an extremely easy to use interface? Do you add in voice commands as standard?

In Fig. 2.4, we can see an unbranded dashboard that can used to send information to both iOS and Android apps. Take note that when sending push notifications (see Glossary), there is the ability to do this with either a sound ping or silently. When the developers were thinking about this part of the functionality and the situation that end users may be in when receiving a notification, they provided the ability to make the push notifications silent. Their thought process was "what if it the system was being used to send information in a dangerous situation, such as a school shooting?" The developers believed lots of phones pinging a noise in such a situation would result in the opposite type of usage of what the administrators with dashboard would want. As a result, they added in the ability to turn off the sound. Since the system has been deployed to real-life towns and citizens, another use of the silent push notification has arisen. Towns can send silent information to their citizens when they believe that the information is not urgent and when they do not want to disturb the citizens, such as at night.

Case Study: Localization

Citizen Alert Inc. is a company that develops mobile apps for small towns.

- www.citizenalert.ca

Although Citizen Alert's target market is English-speaking North America, they built localization into the code base of their apps from the very beginning.

Citizen Alert Inc. is based in Canada, a country which has two official languages: English and French. It also borders the United States of America, which has a lot of Spanish speakers. As a result, considering localization from the beginning was essential.

Citizen Alert Inc. realized that while their main customers were the small towns that would be predominantly English-speaking, it was not much work to build localization into the apps, meaning any of a small town's citizens who use the app could use it in their native language. This would provide a much better end user experience, the citizens of the small towns.

Citizen Alert did this by ensuring that any text-based labels within the app were put into customized strings. Then, keys were used to pull from the correct customized string.

Exercises

Below are a number of exercises to help increase your understanding of the terminology, concepts and material presented in this chapter: Key Ingredients for a Great App.

Exercise No. 2

Write out in one or two sentences what the goal of the app is. Use the example of a To-do-List app.

A good way to start is to think of the app name and what the app is meant to do.

- App Name.................................
- App Goal..................................

Then begin thinking about what the essential or necessary features are and what are the nice-to-have features for the app are. Keep this basic in the beginning.

To-do List App:
- What features are necessary/must have and what are 'nice to have' features.

List out in a table the necessary and the nice-to-have features (Table 2.2).

After completing this simply exercise you will already have a better understanding of your app and the beginnings of insight into the complexity and requirements for the app.

Table 2.2 Showing possible columns to fill in for necessary and nice-to-haves for an app

App Name and Goal	Necessary	Nice-to-have

Exercise No. 3

Write down the Four Ws for the following apps:

- Children's bedtime story app
- Banking app
- Domestic abuse app
- Seniors' community center app
- Gaming app aimed at young adults

App Name..
Who...
Why...
Where...
When..

Notes..

Individual Reflection

To solidify your understanding in 500 words write out what you have learnt from this chapter. Here are some hints that you might use to write about.

- What have you learnt about end users?
- How do different apps have to consider their end user?
- What are the Four Ws
- Give a brief explanation of the Key Ingredients of a Great app.

Knowledge Check

Fill in the blanks of the following sentence:
    Use the words provided in the word bank.

All apps need some .... to make them useful to the end user. Researching the .... will help you understand who your end user is. In the beginning break your app down in to .... and .... When initially designing your app always design for .... then you will know that everyone will be able to use your app. Also including .... from the beginning means that you can easily expanded to different markets in different countries.

Word Bank:
- Key Ingredients, Essential Features, Nice to Have Features, The Four Ws, Discoverability, Accessibility/Inclusivity, Localization.

Answers

Below are suggested answers to the exercise given in this chapter. They are not complete and simply a suggestion to help you further think about your own solutions. You may well come up with a different or better solution. This is part of the app development process.

Exercise No. 2

- App Name: Easy To-Do-List
- App Goal: Provide a simple way for people to jot down to do items.

App Name and Goal	Necessary	Nice-to-have
To-do-list. Easy to use to-do-list for people on the go.	Categorized list of tasks, 'things-to-do'.	
	Linked to calendar	
	Voice capture to add a new task	
		Add a pic to a task
	Add to tomorrow feature	

Exercise No. 3

App Name	Children's bedtime
Who	Adults and young children
Why	To get children to sleep. No flashing or loud sounds
Where	Dimly lit room. Dark mode screen.
When	Late evening, quite relax time

Notes   Getting a story should be very easy, just a few taps as the children may become bored and restless and the parents may be under pressure.

App Name	Bank app
Who	Any person with a bank account
Why	Bank would like to make banking easier for its cliental and also cut down on the need for clients to visit a branch
Where	Multiple locations/places/environments/internet capabilities etc. Localisation important. Also different banking regulations in different countries.
When	All days and times. Different time zones. This should be very clear.
Notes	Privacy on the app screen whilst using the app should be considered. Also, data security a top priority

---

App Name	Domestic abuse app
Who	People under stress maybe seeking help. How people use devices In stressful situations must be consider. Can they swipe effectively. Will they start using the app then have to quickly stop?
Why	Person feels in need of help. Depending on severity of the situation it may impede the users gross motor skills and ability to perform a number of steps in sequence
Where	Home environment or possibly outside in open environment
When	Person has decided to reach out regarding domestic abuse
Notes	Privacy on the app screen whilst using the app should be a top priority. Person using app may be in danger. This must be factored into the app. Maybe the app should NOT look like a domestic abuse app in case the perpetrator sees the app.

App Name	Seniors' Community Center
Who	Elderly people plus maybe the children of elderly people.
Why	Know information about what is happening at their community center
Where	At home, possible slow internet (low bandwidth)
When	Likely during the day – no special requirements
Notes	Accessibility and inclusive design is a top priority with this app.

App Name	Gaming app (high octane)
Who	Likely age range 18 to 60
Why	Seeking entertainment and maybe community. Gaming in teams may be a good idea

Where   At home of Wi-Fi high bandwidth connection.
When   All times of the day and night
Notes   Graphics must be excellent, levels must keep user wanting to play

Knowledge Check Answer

*All apps need some **Key Ingredients** to make them useful to the end user. Researching the **Four Ws** will help you understand who your end user is. In the beginning break your app down in to **Essential Features** and **Nice to Have Features**. When initially designing your app always design for **Accessibility/Inclusivity** then you will know that everyone will be able to use your app. Also including **Localization** from the beginning means that you can easily expanded to different markets in different countries.*

Concept Design

3

Design (which can have many different domains and meanings) is an extremely important part of mobile app development. Here we are talking about 'concept design' or an all-encompassing design that covers many aspects of any app.

Design can sometimes sidelined in favor of coding etc. To learn about the extremely important topic of design for mobile app development, we must appreciate and understand the topic of design as a whole. The key ingredients in Chap. 2: Key Ingredients for a Great App hopefully have given you some insight as to why design is important because we must meet our end users' needs.

Design as a topic covers the 'Big Picture' of the app and how many factors impact the usefulness, usability and success of the app. You will need to think about 'The User Interface (UI)' as being just an important factor as the coding is. You will begin to think about *The User Experience* and what is needed to make the experience of using an app a delight for your end user.

Goal of This Chapter

This chapter will help you understand how to think about the complete design of app. Design will encompass, look, feel, user experience and tools you will need to create an app that has a design that works for the user ender and requirements of the app.

Vocabulary Introduced

- Concept Design
  - Thinking about all the different design aspects of an app. Thinking holistically about design to include many different areas of the app.

T. Salter, *Technological and Business Fundamentals for Mobile App Development*, https://doi.org/10.1007/978-3-031-13855-3_3

- Design thinking
  - Developing an understanding and empathy for the end user.
- Holistic approach
  - Take a broad overview of the project
- User Interface (UI)
  - This is the area which your end user uses to interact with your app
- User Experience (UX)
  - This is the experience that the end user experiences whilst using your app.
- Responsive design
  - These are websites that are programmed in such a way as cleverly adapt to different screen sizes.
- Realism
  - Making the UI appear as close to real objects that we interact with in real life.
- De Facto Standards
  - Something that is a way of doing things whether it is the best way or not.
- User Assistance
  - Designing the UI to helpful to the end user
- Input/Field masking
  - Adding code to make inputting of forms or fields within a form as easy as possible for the end user
- Validation
  - Confirming the accuracy of data that is entered.
- Wireframes
  - The most simple type of visual aid of your app, normally done in just black and white lines.
- Mockups
  - A graphical representation of your app includes more detail and colour than a wireframe.
- Prototypes
  - A representation of your app that can be physically interacted with.

Levels of Understanding

Below in Fig. 3.1 we see a breakdown of knowledge required consider the design of an app. We introduce you to 'design thinking'. In design we include things such as, the look and feel of the app. Does the design help the user easily achieve the goal they have by using the app?

- We see the core knowledge required which covers topics such as understanding how design affects end users.
- Expanded Non-Technical in this area requires a deeper understanding of what is the budget for graphics and branding?
- Expanded Technical knowledge required including a deeper understanding of topics such as how do different design affect how code for the app is written and how different designs affect programming timelines etc.

Expanded Non-technical Understanding	Core Understanding	Expanded Technical Understanding

1. What are the current and future design trends for the target market and end user?
2. How does accessibility affect the end user/design
3. Can the non-technical? team come up with necessary vs nice to have
4. Does non-technical have a basic grasp of how design affects technical?
5. What is the budget for design
  • Graphics
  • Branding
	Concept design
	Understanding design
	Design Thinking
	Responsive Design
	UX in detail
	UI in detail
	Technical design decisions
	Non-technical design decisions
	Mockups
		1. How will different designs affect the overall programming/development of the app?
		2. Can the technical side give realistic timelines/budget for different designs
		3. Can the technical side give design suggestions to non-technical to achieve alternative goals such as cheaper budget/improved UX?
		4. Current best tools for creating a mock-up

Fig. 3.1 Core, Non-Technical and Technical understanding for this chapter

Content

Design Topics in Detail

Below we will look at various design topics in more detail, such as user feedback and accessibility to make sure that any app you oversee or design in the future is perfect for the end user.

User Interface (UI) & User Experience (UX)

These two domains can be whole topics unto themselves. There are companies and occupations that specialize in just UI or just UX design. Each of these domains encompasses a wide range of topics. This book will teach you a basic understanding of what these topics mean. Having a basic understanding of them will help improve any app development you are involved with.

How feature rich or how well the app is coded may not be important to your end user. What may be much more important is:

• How easy is it to use?
• Does it do the job for the end user?
• What is their experience whilst using the app?

UI/UX is about taking the requirements for an app and turning these requirements/features into a design and experience that will achieve these requirements for the end user:

- What is the app meant to do?
- What are the features of the app?
- Who are the end users?

For example, people can lose interest if everything in the app is the same size and colour. Having a good UI/UX means you will get more users, plus your users will be more engaged with your app and more likely to use it. Even minimal UI/UX design will make a big difference to your app. In this section, we will look at some basic things you can do to greatly improve the UI/UX of any app.

Monochrome/Alignment

Begin by designing your interface in a monochromatic colour scheme (black/white) and get the look right without any other design features, such as colour.

- Whether you are using a programming interface or IDE that has a graphical interface or you are using a program to mockup, they will provide alignment guides for you.
- Trust the alignment guides in your graphical interface to make everything look well-aligned and as though a professional designer designed the look of the app (Fig. 3.2).

User Interface (UI)

Everything, from your app store presence to whether users get the right feeling from your app will be affected by the UI. The user interface can be appealing to end users or it can make them move on to a different app. The user interface requires thought to get it right. If you do not have the budget to use professional UI designers, you must at least know the basics to get the look of the app right. The UI should help guide the user to what they want to do. Whether this is checking out when using a

Fig. 3.2 Showing basic text vs. simple formatting

shopping app, adding a new friend in a social media app, or seeing the bonus points available in a game app.

Of course, the type of design you use should depend on your end user. You should understand the end user and be able to make a UI that is suitable for them. Put effort into the details to make the perfect UI for your end users. There are visual tricks that designers use that you can use too. Below you will find some basic UI tricks to use to make your UI a delight for your end user.

When designing the UI for your app, you should consider making it:

- **Intuitive**: The user should instinctively know how to use the app. Recognizable buttons
- **Easy**: The app should be easy to use without instructions.
- **Guide the user**: The user should not have to hunt for what they want. By stylising fonts, the font family and styles, sizes, etc., you can direct the user through your UI.
- **Inviting**: The user should be drawn in to use your app.
- **Functional**: The app works as expected, for examples, buttons, etc.
- **Uncluttered**: There should not be too much information on each screen and there should not be too little information on each screen.
- **Familiar**: Your app should reflect what is familiar to the end user (see Adherence).
- **Realistic**: Try to make your UI have physicality and realism, so that users know what is a button, when a screen is scrollable, etc.. Model your UI after the real world.
- **Appropriate**: The look and feel should be appropriate for the end user, e.g. age group or localised.

User Experience (UX)

UX is about the relationship between end users and computer software products such as websites, apps, etc. You must consider 'what is the user's experience whilst using the software or mobile app?' Creating a great UX for your end users will be an iterative process and to get it right you will need to learn to use tools like Interaction Flow Diagrams, which we discuss later in this section. When thinking about UX try to think about what experience your end user is looking for. Some examples of the experience your end user may be looking for might be:

- Quick (Bank app/messaging app?)
- Secure (Bank app/doctors app?)
- Simple (Senior's app/children's game?)
- Engaging (Gaming app/language learning app?)
- Hidden (Dating app/reporting abuse app?)

When thinking about how to design your app so that it has the UX the end user is looking for, think about the topics in this list:

- Engaging/sticky – the user wants to engage and continue using the app

- Appropriate – whether it is a game or a diet app, does the app give the user the experience they are looking for?
- Work as expected – is everything working, buttons etc.?
- Flow – does the user easily navigate the app or do they get lost in it?

When beginning an overall design experience, list the types of experiences you believe your end user will be looking for. You can list multiple different experiences, for example:

- Quick and secure
- Engaging and fun
- Quick and gets the job done
- Thorough, thoughtful, pleasant

Colour

Colour can be more important than you think. It can set the whole tone for your app. There are two basic decisions you must make regarding colour for your mobile app and logo. (1) picking a base colour and then (2) picking a colour palette from this base colour. These are decisions that you must take seriously. Here, we will help you to understand how colours affect users and why you should put thought into the colours you use. It could affect the success of your mobile app and brand.

Base colours can psychologically invoke different moods/emotions in end users. So you must put thought into the type of mood or emotion you are trying to bring about with your app. This is a list of the moods/emotions that certain colours are thought to typically invoke in Western cultures.

- Red – intensity – love – energy – exciting
- Yellow – joy – attention grabbing – intellect – sunny
- Green – freshness – growth – safety
- Blue – trust – serenity – stability – trustworthy
- Purple – royalty – wealth – feminine (Fig. 3.3)

Other considerations can also be important with colour. Things such as eye strain, should the colour be gentle on the eye if it is being used for a long etc. So when picking a colour note any other factors that should be consider when making your choice.

The emotion or mood brought about by colour can change between cultures. This is something that you must think about also if you are looking for a worldwide market (see Key Ingredient No. 7: Localization).

Here is a colour chart for different cultures produced by toptal.com (Fig. 3.4).

To begin the process of deciding on a colour scheme for your app, begin by picking your base colour. This is the main colour that you will work from. Try to think about what your users will want as a base colour. Then, think about this base colour and the intensity of it. Bold colours work well for children (primary colours), but you may need a more sophisticated colour for adults, maybe not a primary colour

Fig. 3.3 Showing colour. (Source: https://uxstudioteam.com/ux-blog/colour-psychology-in-ux-design/)

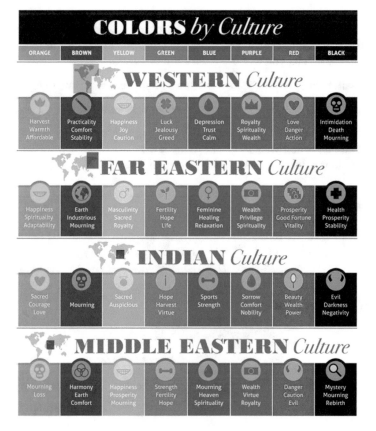

Fig. 3.4 Showing colour. (Source: https://www.toptal.com/designers/ux/colour-psychology)

but a tone of the colour itself instead. Once you have your base colour, you can move on to thinking about a colour palette.

Colour Palettes

Colour palettes help you choose a range of colours for your app based off your initial colour choice. Colour palettes are well-researched and, if you stick with them, you will have a nice looking colour scheme for your app. There are four main colour palettes to choose from. They are:

- Adjacent
  - Colours are next to each other on the colour wheel.
- Complementary
  - Colours are opposite each other on the colour wheel.
- Monochromatic
  - Begin with a base colour and add white or black to change the tone of the colour.
- Split
  - Begin with a base colour and then select the colour that is opposite on the colour wheel, then step one to the right and one to the left, to pick two new colours. In total you will use three colours.

The diagram below shows you how to use and apply colour palettes (Fig. 3.5).

When deciding on a base colour and a colour palette, think:

- What type of app am I developing?
- What emotions do I want to invoke in my users?
- What colour palette will best suit the users and the app?

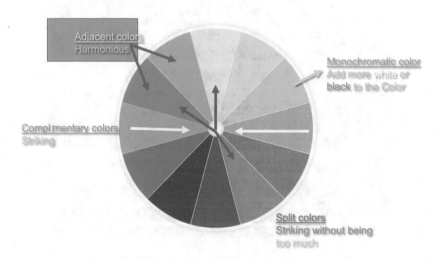

Fig. 3.5 Showing a colour wheel

Typography

It is not just colour that can set the mood or emotion for an app. Having the right font and applying this font in the right way is also important. Fonts can be used to set the mood of an app or they can be used to focus the user's attention on a specific spot on the screen. The font family, size, colour, style and thickness are tools that we can use to set the right mood for the app or to focus attention somewhere on the screen. First, begin by deciding on the type face.

Fonts or typefaces will usually have a set of characters that make up the font family. This typically includes the letters a to z, numbers 0–9, plus symbols, such as punctuation marks. You can then add other characteristics to the font such as size, weight, and style (e.g. italics). Use sites such as Typedia [3] to learn, in detail, about fonts.

There are basic things to consider when choosing the font you will use for your app. Fonts can be broken down into two main categories:

- Sans serif fonts – these are considered more modern
- Serif fonts – these are considered more traditional and serious (Fig. 3.6)

Try to stick to a maximum of two different typefaces mixed together. A good rule to follow if you want to mix different font types, is to have a heading in one font and the body of text in another.

- Serif heading + sans serif body
  - Example Heading in American Typewriter
  - Example body of the text in Calibri.
  - Line two.
  - Line three etc.
- Sans serif heading + serif Body
  Example Heading in Calibri.
  Example body of the text in American Typewriter
  Line two
- Line Three, etc.

The factors you should consider when choosing a font family for your app are things such as:
- Do you need to portray an emotion?
  - Love, anger, joy
- Do you need to convey a certain type of app?
  - Utility, work, leisure, game, calming

Fig. 3.6 Showing the difference between sans serif fonts (left) and serif fonts (right)

- Is the readability of words important?
  - Is safety an issue? Driving, running
  - Is speed reading an issue? Game, music linked to a car dashboard
  - Does the font need to be clear and easy to read? Instructions, lots of text
  - Is the user's ability an issue? Are your users elderly or perhaps dyslexic?
- Device constraints
  - You must consider different screen sizes and people's ability to read on a small screen. You must consider the ability to fit the text under or on a button that can be tapped.
    Will your app be used on a watch?
- Device standards
  - You must also consider the platform's standard font for things such as a back button
- Localization (see Key Ingredient No. 7: Localization)
  - Will the number of letters required be much more in different languages?

Look at the title of the events below, as well as the different font types and colours used. Select what you feel would be the most suitable font for the titles in each of the sections. As well, can you tell which fonts are sans serif fonts and which are serif fonts? The font families are:

1. *Zapfino*
2. **Lucida Blackletter**
3. Desdemona
4. Calibri

Event One

1. *Meeting of the app development team*

2. Meeting of the app development team

3. MEETING OF THE APP DEVELOPMENT TEAM

4. Meeting of the app development team

Event Two

1. A valentines card – all my love

2. A valentines card – all my love
3. A VALENTINES CARD – ALL MY LOVE
4. A valentines card – all my love

Event Three

1. Gaming night entry form

2. Gaming night entry form
3. GAMING NIGHT ENTRY FORM
4. Gaming night entry form

Stylizing fonts

After you have picked a font family to use in your app, you can use different methods to stylize the font. This can help to emphasize something that is important for your user to notice. Below is an example of the two same letters 'UI' stylized in different ways (Fig. 3.7):

ui **ui**   size   ui ui Color   ui **ui** thickness

ui UI CAPITALS   **ui *ui*** italics   ui u i   s p a c i n g

UI *ui* UI   contrast

Fig. 3.7 Various ways to stylize fonts

Icons

Using pictures or icons can sometimes be a better solution rather than using letters or words. This can help with accessibility (see Key Ingredient No. 6: Accessibility/Inclusivity) and also with localization (see Key Ingredient No. 7: Localization). Think about TV remotes that use universal symbols for play, pause, forward and backwards. Using symbols rather than words means that the TV remote manufacturer simply makes one remote for multiple markets. However, you must be careful that your end user understands what the picture/icon means, otherwise you risk simply confusing them.

Which icon below best signifies 'like', as in you like a picture? It can depend on which app you are using (Fig. 3.8).

Ask an elderly person which of the above icons they believe signifies like. Did their choice match your choice?

If you were to decide to use an icon for 'like' rather than the letters to spell the word, you should consider:

- Is there already a standard icon for the word you want to replace?
- Will everyone understand what your icon signifies?

What does the below icon signify? (Fig. 3.9)

Ask an elderly person if they know. The chances are that they do not.

Below is an example of the word 'map' in four different languages,

- (1) English, (2) Italian, (3) Russian, and (4) Chinese.

Which is better: letters or icons? An icon cuts down on the need to localize and also helps with accessibility as long as the end user understands what the icon means. Using well-known icons can work very well. If you invent your own icons, they may not be so well understood (Fig. 3.10).

> It is all very well having all these little pictures in apps but it is no good if I don't understand what they mean! I bet there are millions of people like me.
>   Gary L, Canada. An angry app user.

- Gary L was talking about icons.

Making sure that icons are well known and drawn in such a way as that they are easily recognisable is very important. Your user should easily look at an icon and understand what it represents. Apple offers some great icons, free of charge. To see what Apple is currently recommending for icons and symbols within an app, do an internet search for "Apple developer Human Interface Guidelines Symbols Icons".

Realism

The topic of realism is about attempting to make objects in your app seem like objects in the real world. This will make your app more intuitive to use. Make buttons look like buttons from the real world so the user does not have to guess at

Fig. 3.8 Various icons to represent like

Fig. 3.9 Settings or gear icon

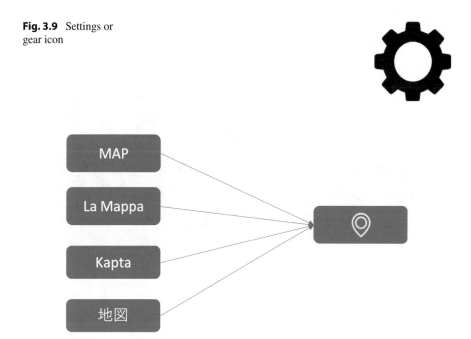

Fig. 3.10 Showing words vs. icon

whether the graphical button on the screen can be tapped or not. This will also help the end user know that something will happen if they do tap the button.

Below is a selection of buttons with increasing graphical techniques applied to make them look like real buttons (Fig. 3.11).

Apple, has pushed the current trend of images in general towards flat images with fewer shadows. Shadows help to make a graphical image appear as though it has depth. Android, on the other hand, has gone from completely flat images towards images that appear to have more depth.

Realism isn't just reserved for buttons or single objects/widgets on the screen. It can be applied to look of the entire app. For example, making a book-reading app really look like a book, or having a user's books displayed on a book shelf rather than just in a list on the screen.

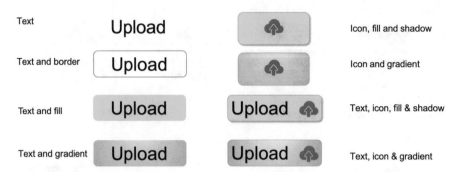

Fig. 3.11   Showing different button formats

Fig. 3.12   Showing realistic book apps. (Source of picture shown in Fig. 3.12: Showing realistic book apps: https://www.quora.com/What-is-the-best-reading-app-and-why#!n=12)

See the images below for examples of how designers and programmers worked together to make realistic apps (Fig. 3.12).

Below in Fig. 3.13: Graphical representation of adding a curl to a page we see a rough depiction of how to add more realism to a reading app. The page curls like the pages of a real book. This is meant to illustrate how the user would use touch to swipe a page rather than pressing a button. This is would perhaps give the user a more delightful, realistic experience.

Delightfulness/Innovation

Try to make your app delightful to the user. Perhaps, this means having a delightful interface, maybe this means an innovation that makes the users' task easier to achieve. Maybe it means that your end user was able to use the app without ever thinking "how do I do X?"

To help make your app delightful to use, think of ways to make things easier for your end user. You can do this by thinking about the small details within your app.

Fig. 3.13 Graphical
representation of adding a
curl to a page

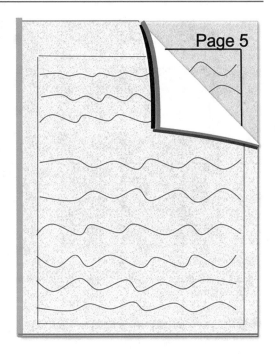

For example, when your app requires the user to enter information, use the correct popup keyboard. For example, if your user needs to enter a phone number make sure you popup the number keyboard. When the user is entering an email address, popup the keyboard with the @ symbol.

When you are designing the UI, make it easy for your end user to know where things are. For example, do not make navigation difficult. Place the back button where the end user would expect it to be. To make things easier for your end user you can also use a technique called field masking or input masking. This technique is covered in more detail later in this chapter (Fig. 3.14).

Desirable

What does desirable mean? It is hard to define what will make your app desirable to the end user. In general, we can say that something that is desired is something that is wanted or wished for. It is why a person picks Car A over Car B. Their choice could be made for a multitude of reasons, perhaps because others perceive Car A to be prestigious. Car A maybe cheaper than Car B whilst still having the same features. Car A maybe available in the right colour. Think of why you have the type of phone you have. Is it because you perceive it to be the best? Is it price? Is it because of the size? What makes it desirable to you? How will you know what is desirable to your end user? Many apps may have the same function or goal, but users will

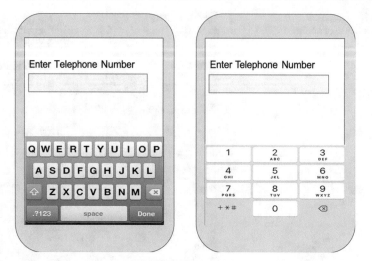

Fig. 3.14 Something as simple as popping up the correct keyboard can help make your app more delightful to use

keep the one that suits their desires. Certainly if your app is more delightful to use it will have an edge over your competition.

Adherence

Use adherence, predictability, consistency and familiarity in your app to help give your end users a pleasant experience whilst using your app. There are various aspects to your app that you can design to be familiar to the end user. What are your end users expecting when they tap a button? Whatever it is, that is what should happen. This is predictability in app terms. Unless you have a very good reason, such as a puzzle game where the user must decipher a puzzle, keep things consistent and predictable. What are some predictable elements within an app?

- Buttons
- Tapping
- Shaking
- Double clicking
- Swiping right

De Facto Standards

These are sometimes called design patterns and they are something that users are used to.

- Example – Pulling the screen down to refresh the page

De facto means being used whether right or wrong. They are things that have become part of everyday life. These too are part of predictability that your users will expect. Can you think of a time that you used what you thought was a de facto standard and it did not generate the outcome that you wanted? The developers should have thought about this. Make sure you adhere to de facto standards.

- Can you think of a 'de facto' standard?
  - Qwerty keyboard
    Swipe right
    Double tap
    It seems there is no consensus on what the de facto standard for shaking a mobile device should be (so it may be wise to avoid using this capability)

Your app should have a consistent feel from screen to screen. The whole look and feel of the app should be consistent, predictable, and intuitive.

- Visual
  - This means having a consistent visual look with regards to fonts, colours, buttons and screen layout. The visual appearance of your app should be consistent throughout the whole app.
- Functional
  - The function and the interactive elements should work the same in all parts of the app. Be consistent in any interactive elements that you use. For example swipe gestures and button navigation should be consistent throughout the app.
- Cross platform
  - Where possible, the design of the app should be consistent across multiple platforms. This can include having the same look and feel on a tablet vs. a small phone and again the same look and feel for iOS vs. Android – although still following manufacturing platform conventions for navigation etc.

Platform Adherence

Try where possible to design for specific platforms. There are certain differences between Apple and Android in the way that UI is laid out and how the navigation happens. Design for the platform (iOS vs. Android). Users will be familiar with the look and feel of the platform and they will expect your app to function this way. They will expect to do things like navigation in a way that is familiar to them. For example, typically navigation is achieved via tab bars in iOS. Whereas navigation is achieved via the hamburger menu in Android. iOS users are used to having a graphical back button that can be tapped on the screen, whereas Android users are used to having the back button be part of the physical hardware. Make sure that you are fully aware of both platforms' differences.

Each platform manufacturer will have certain guidelines that you must adhere to. If you do not adhere to these, you face having your app rejected from their app store or even worse you may face a possible ban.

- To find Apple's design guidelines, search:

- • Human Interface Design Guidelines
- • To find help on Android's design guidelines, search:
  - • Material Design Guidelines.

Look at (Fig. 3.15)

User Assistance

There are various ways you can help your end user out to make using your app simple. There are various techniques that make tasks like filling in user details or forms easier to achieve.

- • Input/field masking

  - • Helping your users with a field in a form
- • Instant feedback

  - • Alerting your users instantly, such as with sounds or colours, to help them use the app correctly
- • Dynamic validation

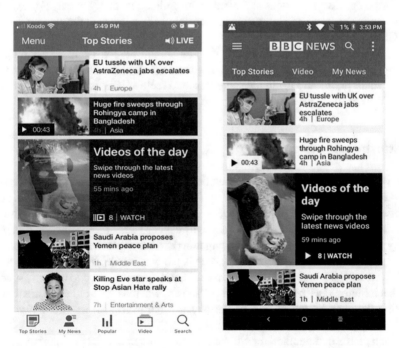

Fig. 3.15 Difference between iOS and Android for the same app

- Instantly checking if data is correct; this is usually done client-side
- Server-side validation
  - Checking data is correct by connecting to a server/database

Input/Field Masking

Mobile device screens can be small, and this can cause difficulties for your user either visually, or physically if they have issues with dexterity abilities. If the user needs to input something in a form, try to make the font as large as possible and use a clear, uncluttered font to help them with visual requirements. Try to keep the amount of information required on one screen to a minimum and use popup keyboards that still leave the part of the form being entered visible.

If it is difficult for the user to enter the information you require, errors may happen and they may give up on your app.

Input or field masking is a way to help users fill in forms. This system will help your user input data correctly. It is a technique that formats the text that the user is inputting to a form.

For example: phone numbers, postcodes, etc. In the code of your app, you can tell it to expect a certain type of text in the form field. For example, the difference between post codes and zip codes is that post codes are typically 3 characters (letters and numbers) followed by a space then a second set of 3 characters (letters and numbers). Whereas a zip code in the USA and countries such as Italy is typically 6 numbers long. You can make sure that your app will only accept characters formatted correctly for the different areas that have either a zip code or a postal code.

Shown below in Fig. 3.16 is an example of a section on Citizen Alert Inc.'s form that is filled out by new customers. New town customers of Citizen Alert must indicate what they would like their app to be called. However, a character limit is placed on the number of characters they can enter as there is a maximum of 12 characters allowed by Apple. The wording inside the box in the input form is coloured in grey, so as, to indicate that the user should type inside the box.

Using Input/field masking will also make collection of the data easier for you as the data will come to you in a format that you are expecting. This means the data will fit nicely into your database. You will not have data that is incorrect, such as a zip code when your database is expecting a postal code.

Shown below in Fig. 3.17 is an example of how to use the correct popup keyboard. Plus, on the right, we see the correct format of a telephone number that the user must enter.

The user will be much happier filling out their telephone number in the right-hand scenario and you will get a correctly formatted telephone number.

Name of App | TownAlert (12 chars max) |

Fig. 3.16 Showing input fields

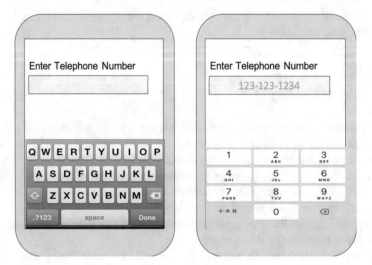

Fig. 3.17 Showing input fields

Data Validation

It is likely that you will, at some point, need to validate some data, whether this be user credentials or stock inventory.

Instant Feedback

It is possible to help your user correctly use your app by giving them instant feedback when something is correct or incorrect. Instant feedback can come in the form of sounds, changes of colour, or image changes (for example a cross or a tick image), see Fig. 3.18. Instant feedback helps your user know that they are using your app in the correct way. Try to give as much instant feedback as you can to your end user. For example, grey out buttons if they are not clickable, then colour the button when it becomes clickable.

Dynamic Validation

In this scenario, you check or validate the user's information instantly. For example, field masking may make sure that the user has entered the 6 numbers required for a zip code, but dynamic validation will check the zip code to confirm that it is a valid zip code. If the user enters 000000 as a zip code, dynamic validation will pick this up and prompt the user to enter a valid zip code.

The difference between 'dynamic validation' and 'validation', is that you validate the data that the user is entering straight away, or you at least break forms up

Fig. 3.18 Showing colour
and images for
accessibility

into small sections and validate the data as soon as you can. This is an added way to help the end user. It can be frustrating for the user if they enter a lot of data in a form and then, when the user presses submit, an error is found and they have to go back through the form. It is a much more pleasant experience for the user if errors are found instantly.

Client-Side Validation and Server-Side Validation

The difference between client-side and server-side validations is where the checking of the data happens. By client-side, we mean that the validation takes place on the user's device. By server-side, we mean that the data travels over a network and the validation takes place on a server (Figs. 3.19 and 3.20).

Whether data is validated client-side or server-side depends on many factors. In this book, we do not go into great detail on this topic. Rather, we wish to give you a basic understanding of the concept so that, if needed, you can go on to examine the topic in more detail. Here, we list some examples for you. However, whether data is validated client or server side will depend on how the system is set-up.

Input values: Has the name been input correctly? For example, checking that only a to z is entered.

Fig. 3.19 Hardware used
in client side

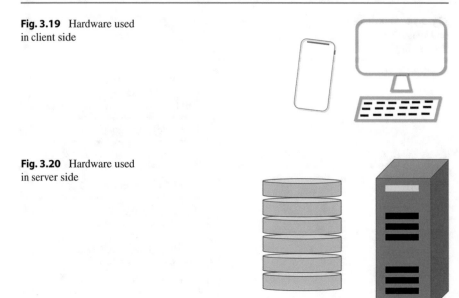

Fig. 3.20 Hardware used
in server side

- This can be handled client-side
  Username: Is it a correct username? Authorizing whether the user has an account
- This is likely to need to be handled server-side
  Inventory: Is that sneaker available in stock?
- This is likely to need to be handled server-side
  Inventory: How many pairs are available?
- This is likely to need to be handled server-side

  Missing values: Did the user enter a number in the 'how many pairs?' section of
the form

- This can be handled client-side
  How you validate data will depend on the project. Be sure you do not violate
DRY – *don't repeat yourself*. Meaning that you do not validate the same data on
both on the client and the server sides (Fig. 3.21).

Future Friendly

You must always consider the future when designing any part of an app. Whether
this be UI or code architecture. In this chapter, we will just consider thinking about
the UI/UX of an app. Look at the picture in Fig. 3.22. Both images are the same app
just with a different UI. The right-hand image looks like a huge improvement, but is
it? What if there were more menu options or more added in the future? What if you

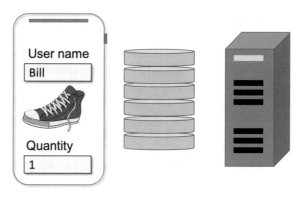

Fig. 3.21 Data can be validated either client side on the mobile device or server side on a server

Version A   Version B

Fig. 3.22 The same app functionality and features with a different design

needed to add some wording? Would it fit? How would people read the wording? If it is left as only icons, would a senior be able to understand the icons? Can you understand all the icons? What are the icons for services, attractions?

Figure 3.22 shows the same app with two different UIs (Version A and Version B). Is the graphical version (Version B) a clear winner?

Research and Development

You must conduct some research and analysis on your app before you upload it to the app stores. You may need to conduct research and then test, analyze your findings, think about how to implement these findings, then test again… You cannot know that the assumptions you make regarding UI/UX, functionality, features etc. will work for your end user unless you test the app out on some of them. You will need to understand how to conduct R&D and how you are going to analyze the results that you collect.

How much time and money you have will affect the amount of research, testing, and redesigning you can do. The more you can design, research, test, and analyze, the better the app will be, but doing this forever is not the answer. You will need to gauge when you have done enough research and when it is time to release the app.

First, you must know who your end user is so that you can find a group of your typical end users and do some research and analysis on them. You can discover your end users by following the instructions given in Chap. 2: Key Ingredients for a Great App, 'The four Ws.'

Once you have a good understanding of your end users, you can make a plan for your R&D. You can think about how you will test your assumptions you made about your app. Think about how you will conduct your research and analysis: What are you trying to find out? How many end users do you think you need as a sample population?

Once you have conducted your research, you must learn from it. You must analyse the data you have collected and learn from your findings. From this, you can see how you can improve the design of your app.

Basic list of things to learn from research and analysis:

- Features
  - Do your users wish there was another feature?
    Would they use all the features you included?
    Is it too feature rich?
- Tasks
  - Can they easily achieve the task they want to do?
    Are there too many steps to achieve the task?
- Entertainment
  - Was the experience enjoyable?
    Would they play the game again?
    Would they use the app again?
- Value
  - Do they see any value in your app? Useful, entertaining, helpful, etc.
    Would they keep the app or delete it?
- UI/UX
  - Is the look and feel of the app suitable for the end user?

After you know your end user well, think about how you will find out the answers to the questions you have. How can you learn from the R & D? How will you test your app on your end user? Will you use a mockup/questionnaire?

Putting It All Together – Practical application

Here we will look at how to put together everything that you have together. In this section, you will apply your new knowledge. You will practice making a user flow diagram and a mockup. You will also get to test out your new skills on a real-life case study. You will be able to compare your newly learnt skills with the award-winning app from the case study. In this book, we also provide you with sheets for you to apply all of your new skills and begin the process of designing and mocking-up an app of your choice.

First, we will show you how to create a user flow diagram and a mockup of an example recipe app. Next, you will create a UI/UX, user flow diagram, and a mockup of a real-life case study. Finally, you will create a UI/UX, user flow diagram, and a mockup for an app of your choice.

Overall Design

Design is an essential element of all mobile app development. Great coding or a great app idea will not be successful without a design element applied to the app.

There are many different factors that go into a well-designed app, including colours, fonts, interaction flow, User Interface (UI) and User Experience (UX) Design. Whether you are doing the design yourself, or overseeing a designer, you will need to understand good design principles.

When it comes to design, there are some basic simple rules for you to follow. This book will explain these rules to you. If you are doing all the work yourself and follow these rules, the design element will make your app look like it has a cohesive, well-thought-out design and purpose. If you are overseeing designers, you will understand if they are making good decisions about the design of your app. Design can make or break the app.

To begin with, you must learn to think about the picture of your app: look at the domain the app falls within and think about your end users.

It's important to learn to let go of our own assumptions about the product. We all apply own biases to things – for example, what do you think of when you think of a cat? What you think of might not be the same as what another person thinks.

- A cat is…
  - Person A: Fluffy, cute, companion, family
    Person B: Allergies, scratching, hair, damage to home

Fig. 3.23 Time
assignment for developing
just the app

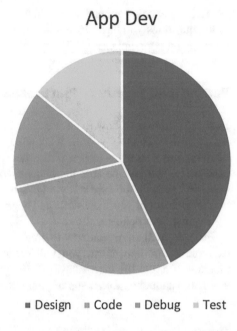

To create a successful app, you must learn to drop your own biases and find out what your end user will think of your app. You cannot instinctively know what your user will want or know how they will use your app.

The above (Fig. 3.23: Time assignment for developing just the app) is not meant to be an exact recommendation. The figure is meant to give you a visual representation to show you that there is a lot more to even the technical development of an app other than just coding.

Design vs. Function

You may want to design something a certain way because it looks nice (design), but your app's users may choose to use it in a different way (function). A standard rule in app design is prioritize *function* before *design.* This may seem like a contradiction when 'design' is being emphasized in this chapter so heavily, but this book will teach you how to *design* for your users' *function* first. So, you will learn to design an app that looks and feels great to the user, but also functions in a manner that they will want.

Apple has previously suggested to think in large terms or in an overview when first designing an app. They suggest thinking about the app in these terms at the beginning of the design process. Below in Fig. 3.24: Showing a way to use a large scale categorize your app, we see how you can think of your app in broad terms of entertainment or utility/work.

Fig. 3.24 Showing a way to use a large scale categorize your app

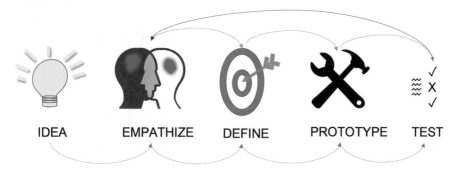

Fig. 3.25 Showing an iterative design process

Iteration

Design is not a one-step process. You must *learn to learn*, things along the way. You must understand that you will need to go back and adjust your app as you learn more about your user and make discoveries about the app (Fig. 3.25).

Stanford has a whole school dedicated to thinking about design called *d.school*. You can see the school's website at: https://dschool.stanford.edu/

They tell us…

> *Design thinking revolves around a deep interest in developing an understanding of the people for whom we're designing the products or services. It helps us observe and develop empathy with the target user. Design thinking helps us in the process of questioning: questioning the problem, questioning the assumptions, and questioning the implications. Design thinking is extremely useful in tackling problems that are ill defined or unknown, by reframing the problem in human-centric ways, creating many ideas in brainstorming sessions, and adopting a hands-on approach in prototyping and testing. Design thinking also involves ongoing experimentation: sketching, prototyping, testing, and trying out concepts and ideas.*

1. **Empathize** – *think as though you are the end user*
2. **Define** – *your users' needs, their problem, and your insights*
3. **Ideate** – *by challenging assumptions and creating ideas for innovative solutions*
4. **Prototype** – *to start creating solutions*
5. **Test** – *solutions*

Stanford notes "*It is important to note that the five phases, stages, or modes are not always sequential. They do not have to follow any specific order.*"

Mockups (see Wireframes/Mockups/Prototypes)

- What type of mockup will you use?
- How will you test it with the end user?
- Online, in-person trials?

When you conduct your R&D it is likely to be an iterative process, you will likely need to carry this out more than once. Your end users will give you insight into how to improve your app. Your time will not be wasted if you conduct good R&D.

Design: Trust

You have probably never thought about trust as an important part of app development. But as security and privacy become an increasingly hot topic, trust between your app and the end user may be key. It is a good idea to strategically plan when you ask for permissions for things such as using a user's GPS coordinates.

Wait to run popups that ask for permissions until you need them. The user doesn't know your app at the beginning and therefore may be wary of giving you any access or privilege to their personal data. Therefore, it may not be wise to popup all the permissions you may need at the first launch of the app. If you can, give the user time to know that you are credible. If you can, wait to ask for permissions until the app actually needs them. Using incremental requests for permissions will build up trust with your end user.

Accessibility and Inclusive Design

The terms 'accessibility' or 'inclusive design' are used to cover the process of making software of all types including apps and websites that are accessible or usable by everyone. Everyone of all different abilities should be considered for the developers design decisions. By not considering the use of inclusive design in your overall design decisions, you run lots of different risks. There will be the possibility of losing end users or maybe having disappointed end users rating your app poorly.

Always consider accessibility in any type of software/app development that you do. If you design for accessibility you know that everyone will be able to use your app. When you are going through the design process and looking at UI/UX, think about the differently abled: hearing, vision, dexterity, age or learning impaired.

How many of your users are likely to be colour blind? Colour blindness (Colour vision deficiency, or CVD) affects approximately 1 in 12 men (8%) and 1 in 200 women in the world [4].

- Red and green are the colours most affected by CVD

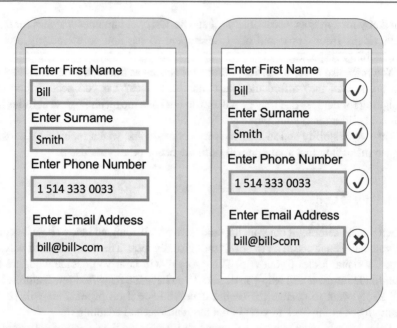

Fig. 3.26 Accessibility for those who are colour blind

Have you seen this on a digital form… "The fields marked in red are required"? Try not to rely on colour as the only feedback for your users.

Look at Fig. 3.26: Accessibility for those who are colour blind below. The right-hand image uses accessibility or inclusive design. The designers considered that not everyone can see the colours red and green distinctly.

Generally when designing, use the following list as the bare minimum of thought that you build into the app to accommodate people that may have accessibility issues:

- Buttons to increase font sizes for people with vision problems
- Text to speech for people with vision problems
- Colour blindness
- Using multiple forms of feedback (visual images, colour, sounds)
- Taking the elderly into account
- Dexterity. Realizing that people may have motor skills issues making it hard to achieve the swipe gesture you spent hours implementing

Accessibility is now a legal obligation in lots of countries, such as within the EU and also in smaller jurisdictions such as Ontario, Canada. If you design with accessibility in mind, you will increase your market share and not be caught out by legal obligations.

At the time of printing this textbook Apple currently provides you will an Accessibility Inspector within Xcode that will help you with the task of checking

whether your app is as 'accessible' as it can be. Carry out internet searches for reputable videos from Apple and other developers to see how to effectively use the Accessibility Inspector.

You may also need to consider other factors such as the economic status of your end users. Can they afford the latest mobile devices? Do you need to consider designing for devices that may be old and do not have the technological abilities that you are building into your app?

Take accessibility and inclusivity very seriously and watch reputable videos on how to make sure that your app will fulfil the needs of all your users.

Visual First Look

When you have thought out your app and have a well-rounded idea of how it should be, you can then proceed on to how it will visually look. There are different ways to obtain a visual look of your app. This process will help you decide what are the essential features. It will help you decide if you have too many/too few features. You will likely want to change the design once you see it on paper. This will be the beginning of going back to your initial assumptions and adapting it.

There are two main ways to get your first insight into the design of your app: by using User Flow Diagrams and by creating a visual representation. While there are different methods used for visually seeing your design, the general term most often used is a *Mockup*.

Before you use either of these methods (User Flow Diagram or Mockup), begin by deciding on the minimum number of features needed to accomplish your app (This chapter: *Concept Design*). Cut everything else out so that you have a very basic app.

Why make a user flow diagram or mockup?

- Save time
- Possibly save you money
- Allow you to redo things
- Avoid miscommunications with: clients/bosses/team members/investors, etc.
- Ensure everyone has the same vision for the app (on the same page)
- Check with potential users (Is it what they want?)

This is more important that what it seems at the moment.

From these processes you get a visual of how the app will look for each view/page. It will help you break up your code into various parts

- Widgets/buttons
- Screens/pages
- Navigation
- User data
- Types of data required

User Flow Diagrams

User flow diagrams show a basic outline of the user's journey through your app. They help you to think about how the end user will navigate through your app. User flow diagrams will help you think about the user's experience using your app. They will help you understand what experience your end user will have whilst trying to complete a task. They will help you realise if there are too many steps required to achieve something.

User flow diagrams are made up of a simple square to denote a screen and a diamond to denote a user action, with arrows in between them. Typically, you will pick a single task at a time and map it out with the user flow diagram. Do not attempt to create a user flow diagram for the whole app as it will be too complex and will not help you to see if any one task is too complicated or not.

We will go over examples in the third section of this chapter for practice. We will show you how to use user flow diagrams in an example case study. This will help walk you through the process of using user flow diagrams. Below in Fig. 3.27: The main components of Flow Diagrams we see an example of a user flow diagram (Fig. 3.28).

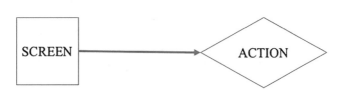

Fig. 3.27 The main components of Flow Diagrams

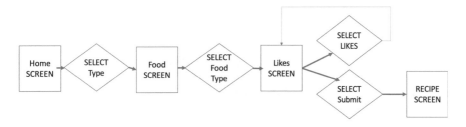

Fig. 3.28 The flow for a recipe app

Wireframes/Mockups/Prototypes

All apps begin life in a wireframe/mockup/prototype stage. This is a representation of the final product. You can think of it just like a house begins with blueprints, then often progresses on to a graphical representation, followed by a show home. The blueprint, graphical representation, and show home are all representations of the actual house that will someday be someone's home.

There are various types of mockups. These begin with using a pencil and paper to sketch your design, then progressing all the way to coded prototypes. You should always begin with a simpler type of mockup. Begin on paper or PowerPoint and progress on to other forms; this that will help you create a more realistic mockup to finally prototypes laid out in an IDE.

Here is a list of different ways/platforms to create a visual representation:

- Simple drawing/White board
- Stencils
- Pads
- PowerPoint
- Drawing software of choice
- Software designed to make mockups
- IDE

In app development, we follow the same path - beginning simple and getting more complex.

There are various ways to visually see your design. These begin with sketching on paper and go all the way to coded prototypes. You should always begin with a simple method. Here are three names of the main types of methods

- Wireframe
- Mockup
- Prototype

The most simple method to see your design is named a: **Wireframe**

- No colour, just thinking about the basic on each view
- Sketch
- Beginning

Below we see some of the tools you can use to create a wireframe (Figs. 3.29 and 3.30).

Next, we progress on to a more graphical representation named a: Mockup

- Based off approved wireframe
- Add colour, graphics, maybe sounds
- More realistic, more detail (Fig. 3.31)

To create a mockup, you can use anything from Paint to PowerPoint to get started on a basic level. There are lots of free templates of the objects/widgets that are used

Fig. 3.29 Wireframe being developed on a white board. (Source: https:// userguiding.com/blog/ wireframe-design/)

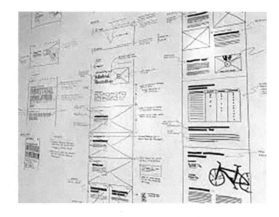

Fig. 3.30 Sketch Pad. (https://mark-anthony.ca/ product/ ui-ux-sketch-pad-sheets/)

in iOS and Android. Then, there is a whole host of free, paid for, desktop, mobile, Android and Apple resources available to help you make a great graphical mockup.

Then, finally you produce a: Prototype.

Both Apple (Xcode) and Android (Android Studio) provide graphical interfaces where you can make the UI/UX of your app.

- Test on computer/device/simulator (Fig. 3.32)

To finalize this chapter, we will recap the ideas that we attempted to put across to you.

Use very simple design techniques to improve the app for your end users.

- Consider things such as:
  - Colours/fonts
    Wording vs. icons
    Realism
    Accessibility
    Assisting the end user
    Data validation

Fig. 3.31   Various app available to make mockups

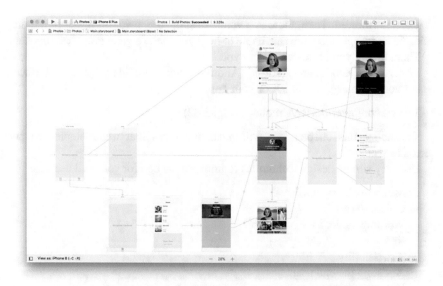

Fig. 3.32   Prototype. (Source: https://matteomanferdini.com/ios storyboards-xcode/)

Research and analysis
Trust
Adherence

Always use user flow diagrams and mockups to test your ideas
A little bit of work built into the beginning of the app will go a long way!

Chapter Summary

Think about everything you have learnt about designing a mobile app. What do you remember? Can you think about the big picture of designing an app? Can you remember any of the topics in more detail? When you have a great idea for an app, will you be able to think it through using all the useful tools you have learnt?

Remember to follow the steps below, but not necessarily in this order:

1. List the four Ws – show that you understand your users' needs
2. Features – necessary vs. nice-to-have
3. UI/UX – what is the right UI/UX for your project?
4. Create a user flow diagram and a mockup
5. Test with a person. Can they work out how to use your app?
6. Iterate, iterate, iterate and learn!

Further Reading

To make sure that you are up-to-date and keeping up with current trends and development techniques carry out searches for the following terms:

- The differences between iOS & Android Design
- Understanding typography
- Reviews of eye dropper extensions for web browsers
- Learning about user flow diagrams
- Learning about wireframes, mockups and prototyping
- Graphics programs
- iOS resources for developing mobile apps
- Android resources for developing mobile apps

Always be sure to check that the resources you are using is reputable and up-to-date.

Case Study – Citizen Alert Inc.

Look at the base colour and colour palette for the app below:

- What base colour and colour palette did the developers decide to use?
- Why did they use these?

Fig. 3.33 Showing colour selection for an app

- Why is the 'Call' button red?
- Do their choices work? (Fig. 3.33)

Initial list of features

- Branded
- Notifications
- Alerts
- Customizable Town
- Customizable End User
- Their target market
- Focus of their system
- Extra functionality/Features
- Two-way communication
- Geo-fencing
- Multilingual

- Registration
- Integrations

Exercises

Below are a number of exercises to help increase your understanding of the terminology, concepts and material presented in this chapter: *Concept Design.*

Exercise No. 4

Pick a colour palette for the following apps.
    A children's learning app.
- Base colour…………………………..
Colour palette ……………………….
A fast-paced game.
- Base colour…………………………..
Colour palette ……………………….
A health centre app. (Use a real health center's logo for reference)
- Base colour…………………………..
Colour palette ……………………….
A bank app. (Use a real bank's logo for reference)
- Base colour…………………………..
Colour palette ……………………….
A word puzzle.
- Base colour…………………………..
Colour palette ……………………….
A flower shop.
- Base colour…………………………..
Colour palette ……………………….

Exercise No. 5

Pick a font(s) for the following apps:

A children's learning app.	Font name ……………………………
A fast-paced game.	Font name ……………………………
A health center app.	Font name ……………………………
A bank app.	Font name ……………………………
A word puzzle game.	Font name ……………………………
A flower shop	Font name ……………………………

Combine the colour palette and font(s) chosen. Write three keywords for the app in the colour palette and font typeface you have selected from Exercises No. 2 & 3.

Exercise No. 6

A children's learning app.	Word 1............... Word 2............ Word 3..............
A fast-paced game.	Word 1............... Word 2............ Word 3..............
A health centre app.	Word 1............... Word 2............ Word 3..............
A bank app.	Word 1............... Word 2............ Word 3..............
A word puzzle game.	Word 1............... Word 2............ Word 3..............
A to-do list.	Word 1............... Word 2............ Word 3..............

How many words could be replaced by icons? ....
Are they well-known icons? ....

Exercise No. 7

Now try replacing at least one word with a suitable icon for each app.

A children's learning app.	Word 1............... Word 2............ Icon....................
A fast-paced game.	Word 1............... Word 2............ Icon....................
A health center app.	Word 1............... Word 2............ Icon....................
A bank app.	Word 1............... Word 2............ Icon....................
A word puzzle game.	Word 1............... Word 2............ Icon....................
A to-do list.	Word 1............... Word 2............ Icon....................

Think about whether your choices work? Who would your choices work for: Everyone, young people? Ask someone if they know what the icon you chose means. Does their answer match the word you chose to replace? Can the elderly person understand your icon? Do you like the end result? Does anything need adjusting?

Exercise No. 8

To further your understanding of how different apps have different requirements, complete the following exercise.

List all the differences between the iOS and Android app seen in Fig. 3.15: Difference between iOS and Android for the same app. Include differences in navigation, fonts, colours, buttons, etc.

Navigation	iOS...........................	Android......................
Fonts	iOS...........................	Android......................
Colours	iOS...........................	Android......................
Buttons	iOS...........................	Android......................
Others	iOS...........................	Android......................

Exercise No. 9

In Fig. 3.22: The same app functionality and features with a different design. We see the same app functionality but with a different UI and UX. List two reasons why Version B may NOT be superior to Version A.
* Reason 1...
Reason 2 ....

Exercise No. 10

Write down a basic features list and the four Ws for the following apps:

* Children's bedtime story app
* Banking app
* Domestic abuse app
* Seniors' community center app
* Gaming app aimed at young adults

App Name and Goal	Necessary	Nice-to-have
Children's bedtime story app		
Banking app		
Domestic abuse app		
Seniors' center app		
Gaming app		

Projects

In this section of this chapter: *Concept Design* you will have two different exercises (Exercise No. 11 and Exercise No. 12). These exercises could be considered projects. Firstly, you will actually move through the process of creating an app to the mockup stage. Remember the steps you have learned so far and go through the process of creating a recipe app, from idea to testing. We list them below as a reminder. Next, you will be given an exercise that could be based on a real-life case study. You will be given the specifications of the required app. You must produce.

We will follow this process:

1. Idea/concept
2. The four Ws
3. Features
4. UI/UX
5. User flow diagram
6. Mockup
7. Testing

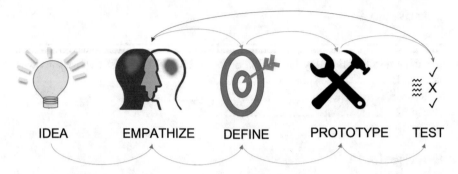

IDEA   EMPATHIZE   DEFINE   PROTOTYPE   TEST

Fig. 3.34 Iterative design process

Do not forget, this is not a one-step process. You must 'learn to learn' things along the way – to go back and adjust your app to your user. Therefore, as you go through this process, go back and visit different parts to see if you can improve on them (Fig. 3.34).

Exercise No. 11

Make your own version of the cooking app.
  Imagine you have been given a brief to develop a cooking app.

- What is the big picture scale for your cooking app (see Fig. 3.24: Showing a way to use a large scale categorize your app)?
- What are your biases about a cooking app?
- Who is the end user? (Who)
- What do they want from using the app? (Why)
- What experience are you hoping to create for the user? (Features, Where and When)
- What should the UI look like?
- What colour scheme?
- What fonts?

1. Idea – an app that lets the end user pick a type of food and get recipes with ingredients and instructions.
2. List out the four Ws
     (i) Who
    (ii) Why
   (iii) When
   (iv) Where
3. List out the features

   (i) Think about the UI/UX – how will it look?

   (ii) Necessary

   (iii) Nice-to-Have

4. Create a user flow diagram and mockup

5. Iterate and learn!

Exercise No. 12

In March 2020 much of the world became aware of a virus named COVID-19. At time of publication of this book the world had being dealing with COVID-19 for over 2 years. The World Health Organisation tells us this about COVID-19 [5].

Coronavirus disease (COVID-19) is an infectious disease caused by the SARS-CoV-2 virus.

Most people infected with the virus will experience mild to moderate respiratory illness and recover without requiring special treatment. However, some will become seriously ill and require medical attention. Older people and those with underlying medical conditions like cardiovascular disease, diabetes, chronic respiratory disease, or cancer are more likely to develop serious illness. Anyone can get sick with COVID-19 and become seriously ill or die at any age.

The best way to prevent and slow down transmission is to be well informed about the disease and how the virus spreads. Protect yourself and others from infection by staying at least 1 metre apart from others, wearing a properly fitted mask, and washing your hands or using an alcohol-based rub frequently. Get vaccinated when it's your turn and follow local guidance.

The virus can spread from an infected person's mouth or nose in small liquid particles when they cough, sneeze, speak, sing or breathe. These particles range from larger respiratory droplets to smaller aerosols. It is important to practice respiratory etiquette, for example by coughing into a flexed elbow, and to stay home and self-isolate until you recover if you feel unwell.

Governments around the world grappled with how to handle the outbreak. They imposed measures in an attempt to manage COVID-19; measures which drastically altered the day-to-day life of many people. One of the measures put in place by a large number of countries was 'Stay at home orders' [6]. These orders restricted the movement of people in an attempt to stop the spread of COVID-19. Some believed these measures were essential to beat the new virus that was spreading around the world [7].

One unforeseen negative consequent of restrictions being imposed on people's lives was an increase in domestic violence [8]. Domestic violence covers a range of violations that happen in a domestic space such as a home. This term encompasses intimate partner violence (IPV), a form of abuse that is perpetrated by a current or ex-partner [9]. Bradbury-Jones & Isham tell us *"Through all of that, children and their mothers are particularly vulnerable (End Violence against Children, 2020) to the risk of domestic violence"* [9]. It seems that cases of domestic violence increased quite rapidly in various countries around the world as a negative consequence of COVID-19 restrictions that were put in place.

Thinking of technology as a means to help those suffering from domestic abuse may not be a natural conclusion. In fact, we often hear news reports about abusers using technology to track or stalk victims of abuse. WebMD has written an article about abusers using technology against their victims [10]. The British Police have issued guidelines on what to do if you call 999 (911 in other countries) but are unable to speak. The guidelines can be found here [11].

It also appears that many others have also found ingenious ways to use technology to help those in need. One year after much of the world knew about COVID-19 in March 2021 a journalist (Adam Easton) from the BBC (British Broad Casting) wrote an article on the increase of domestic abuse during the Coronavirus pandemic COVID-19 [12]. The title of the article was "Why this teen set up a fake cosmetic shop". This article gave us a valuable insight into how technology can be used in very unexpected ways. The article writes about a 17 year old Polish girl who set up a fake cosmetic shop for those suffering from domestic abuse. The idea is that those suffering abuse can use the website to secretly ask for help. Something that may be surprising is that at the time that Easton wrote the article 10% of people requesting help were men. The majority of the victims contacting the website were under the age of 40.

The BBC (British Broadcasting Company) produced a very interesting video on the topic of domestic abuse during COVID-19. It was available on the BBC's news website.

If it is possible to still see the BBC video on domestic abuse or after watching this video or other material and/or researching the topic of domestic abuse further consider how you could develop an app for domestic abuse victims. Will the app need to be simple? What creative ideas can you come up with so as to ensure the victim will not be placed in more danger due to using your app?

After watching the video mentioned above or after watching other material or perhaps researching the topic of domestic abuse further. Consider how you could develop an app for domestic abuse victims. Will the app need to be simple? What creative ideas can you come up with so as to ensure the victim will not be placed in more danger due to using your app?

- Design the first two pages for a victim abuse support app. Imagine that your end user is someone suffering domestic abuse during a government lockdown.
- Write out the four Ws. How can you get to know this particular end user? Will there be challenges in get information from the end user considering their current circumstances. Will you need to speak organizations that deal with domestic abuse?
- What functionality, features should be in the app – specific things about a domestic abuse app
- How can you assist or help the end user?
- What colour palette, font(s) would you use?
- Innovation! What innovation can you bring to this app?
- Make a basic user flow diagram for the two pages and a basic mockup (Fig. 3.35).

Fig. 3.35 FaceBook page for a site to assist domestic abuse victims

Individual Reflection

To solidify your understanding in 500 words write out what you have learnt from this chapter. Here are some hints that you might use to write about.

- How does design affect apps?
- What is the difference between a user flow diagram and a wireframe?
- Why is understanding the Four Ws so important?

Knowledge Check

Fill in the blanks of the following sentence:
  Use the words provided in the word bank.
  There are multiple different tools to help design the UI & UX of an app. You can use .... to see how actions and screens link together and you can use various forms of .... to see a visual representation of the app. When deciding on which keyboard to pop up you should always consider .... to make it as easy as possible for the user. Implementing .... Also makes it easier for the user to know what to input into a form.

Word Bank:
- User Flow Diagrams, Wireframes, Mockup, Prototype, Input/Field masking, User assistance,

Answers

Below are suggested answers to the exercise given in this chapter. They are not complete and simply a suggestion to help you further think about your own solutions. You may well come up with a different or better solution. This is part of the app development process.

Exercise No. 4

Pick a colour palette for the following apps.

   A children's learning app.
- Base colour: Primary colours base (Orange)

Colour palette: Split colours

A fast-paced game.
- Base colour: Vivid colours base (Bright Green)

Colour palette: Complimentary

A health centre app. (Use a real health center's logo for reference)
- Base colour: Easy on the eye base (Blue for trust)

Colour palette: Monochromatic

A bank app. (Use a real bank's logo for reference)
- Base colour: Bank's brand colours

Colour palette: Harmonious

A word puzzle.
- Base colour: Simple, easy on the eye base (Soft Green)

Colour palette: Complimentary

A flower shop.
- Base colour: Pink, pastel colours

Colour palette: Harmonious

Exercise No. 5

Pick a font(s) for the following apps:

A children's learning app.	Font name: Arial in case of any disabilities.
A fast-paced game.	Font name: Courier, easy to read (for quickness) but slightly different to add interest
A health center app.	Font name: Gill Sans Mt., It is wide spaced and easy to read
A bank app.	Font name: Would follow their branding
A word puzzle game.	Font name: Ayuthaya, easy to read but slightly different and more fun
A flower shop	Font name: Apple Chancery to give a sense of feminine

Combine the colour palette and font(s) chosen. Write three keywords for the app in the colour palette and font typeface you have selected from Exercise No. 4 and Exercise No. 5.

Exercise No. 6

A children's learning app.   Word 1 Words Word 2 Numbers Word 3 Objects

A fast-paced game.   Word 1 Level Word 2 Score   Word 3 Lives Left

A health centre app.   Word 1 Welcome Word 2 Appointment Word 3 Information

A bank app.   Word 1 *Sign In* Word 2 *Accounts* Word 3 *Transfers*

A word puzzle game.   Word 1 Guess   Word 2 Hint   Word 3 Leader Board

A flower shop   Word 1 Bouquets Word 2 Order   Word 3 Delivery

How many words could be replaced by icons?

Are they well-known icons? Some such as a plus sign and in a to-do-list app this many be very common.

Add in as many as you can.

Exercise No. 7

Now try replacing at least one word with a suitable icon for each app.

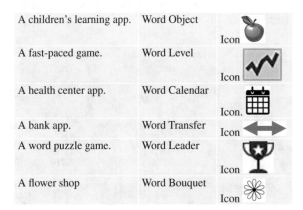

Think about whether your/the authors choices work? Who would your choices work for: Everyone, young people? Ask someone if they know what the icon you chose means. Does their answer match the word you chose to replace? Can the

elderly person understand your icon? Do you like the end result? Does anything need adjusting?

Exercise No. 8

List all the differences between the iOS and Android app's seen in Fig. 3.15: Difference between iOS and Android for the same app. Include differences in navigation, fonts, colours, buttons, etc.
- Navigation: iOS Tab Bar, Android Hamburger Menu
Android has extra navigation bar under top heading bar
Android has black bottom bar
iOS has white tab bar navigation
iOS shows pictures of five stories
Android shows pictures of four stories
Cannot see LIVE on Android
Slightly larger sans serif font used on Android

Exercise No. 9

In Fig. 3.22: The same app functionality and features with a different design. We see the same app functionality but with a different UI and UX. List two reasons why Version B may NOT be superior to Version A.
- Reason 1: If the categories of the app are extended they may not all fit within the graphical circle
Reason 2: All of the icons may not be easily understood and the text inside the inner circle may be too small to be read.

Exercise No. 10

- Children's bedtime story app
- Banking app
- Domestic abuse app
- Seniors' community center app
- Gaming app aimed at young adults

App name and goal	Necessary	Nice-to-have
Children's bedtime story app	Stories by age range	Computer read out loud
	Stories by genre	Different voices for read out loud
	Stories for special occasions e.g. birthday, Christmas, Passover etc	Stories in different languages
		Computer read out loud in different languages?

App name and goal	Necessary	Nice-to-have
		Stories where you can insert the child's name(s)
Banking app	Clients account information	Credit score information
	Transfer money by e-transfer; worldwide	Financial suggestions
	Change personal details; address etc Apply for credit	Live chat button for help
Domestic abuse app	Easy way to communicate	Connection to local area services such as support centers
	Disguised UI	
	Very simple layout	
	Live: chat by text or voice	
	Low data usage in case user is using app in difficult connection area	
Seniors' center app	Simple clear UI/UX. Navigation must have at most three steps.	Increase text size. Voice over.
	No complicated swipe gestures	
Gaming app	Vibrant UI. Great graphics,	Different backgrounds either by choice or based on localisation
	Fast paced UX feeling	Geo location teams

Exercise No. 11

Idea

- An app that easily lets you pick a type of food and get recipes with ingredients and instructions. The focus of the app is ease and quickness, rather than being loaded with features.

The Four W's

1. Who (end user)

   (a) Adult
   (b) Gender neutral
   (c) Might be worried about weight/appearance/health or dietary requirements
   (d) Living in English-speaking countries (but want to expand)
   (e) Does geolocation affect access to ingredients?

2. When

   (a) Afternoon/Evening

3. Why

   (a) They need help with making dinner
   (b) They need to know the ingredients
   (c) They need instructions
   (d) They lack time

(e) They lack knowledge/idea for recipes

(f) They may have dietary requirements

4. Where

   (a) At home

   (b) Kitchen

      (i) Sticky hands

      (ii) Wet

      (iii) Not able to hold a phone (innovation?)

      (iv) Text larger??? (innovation?)

      (v) Text to Speech??? (innovation?)

   (c) Wi-Fi

   (d) At grocery store getting ingredients – cell data signal

- Features

  - Select preferred food (necessary)
  - Select recipe based on health/diet/requirements (necessary)
  - Select recipe based on time (necessary)
  - Select likes (ingredients) (necessary)
  - See recipes (necessary)

    - Ingredients
      Instructions

  - Recipes based on GPS (nice-to-have)
  - Recipes based on regions (nice-to-have)
  - Favorite recipes (necessary)
  - Text to speech (necessary)
  - Large text (necessary)

- UI

  - Gender neutral
  - In English (expanding to Spanish at later date)
  - Fun, easygoing, simple interface
  - Easy to read (not holding phone)
  - Font: Comic Sans, because fun but still easy to read and good for those with dyslexia
  - Colour: Green – gender neutral, freshness (food), monochromatic palette for ease

- UX

  - Quick
  - Simple
  - Easy to use/Clear
  - No fuss, get the job done
  - Less features to create an easy UX

- Big Picture – on the scale, I have placed the app towards entertainment but not too far because I feel the app has a job to do and must be useful. Considering the placement of the overall app on this scale will help when designing the UI and UX (Fig. 3.36).

Exercise 11: User Flow Diagrams (Fig. 3.37)

User flow diagram showing a user selecting a new recipe (Fig. 3.38).

This action of selecting a receipt requires the end user to take a minimum of 4 actions before getting to a recipe. Is this suitable? Would it be ok for there to be more steps? Are there too many steps? User trials would help with gaining this knowledge.

Fig. 3.36 Example of rating an app on a scale

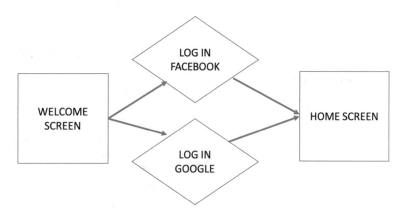

Fig. 3.37 Login shown in a User Flow Diagram

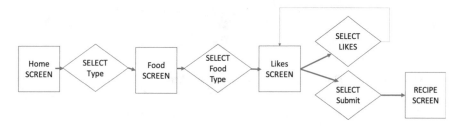

Fig. 3.38 User Flow Diagram for a recipe app

Exercise 11: Mockup (Fig. 3.39)

Exercise 11: Mockup connected to User flow diagram

Below we see Fig. 3.40: How a User Flow Diagram and Mockup fit together which shows the user flow diagram in conjunction with the mockup.

Would this app be successful on an app store? As it stands, it is very doubtful. How can you change/improve on this version of the app?

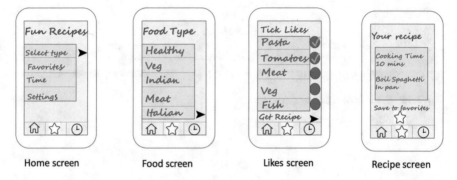

Fig. 3.39 Mockup of a recipe app

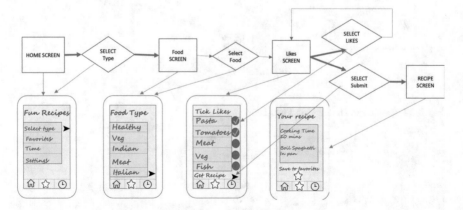

Fig. 3.40 How a User Flow Diagram and Mockup fit together

Case study answer

- What base colour and colour palette did the developers decide to use?

  - Blue and monochrome
- Why did they use these?

  - Blue invokes trust and it was felt that users needed to trust the services being provided by the app
- Why is the 'Call' button red?

  - It was originally designed as an emergency call button
- Do their choices work?

  - The call button colour and name needed to be changed as time went on because it turned into a 'contacts – for emails, departments etc' button

Knowledge check answer

There are multiple different tools to help design the UI & UX of an app. You can use **User Flow Diagrams** *to see how actions and screens link together and you can use various forms of* **Wireframes, Mockups and Prototypes** *to see a visual representation of the app. When deciding on which keyboard to pop up you should always consider* **User Assistance** *to make it as easy as possible for the user. Implementing* **Input/Field Masking** *also makes it easier for the user to know what to input into a form.*

Technology & Technical Development

4

The aim of this chapter is to help you *understand the fundamentals of app development technology* or, to put it another way, *understand the fundamentals of the technology that you can use to develop an app.* This chapter will introduce you to the different kinds of apps that exist and the different programming languages, environments, and ways to technologically create an app.

As with the rest of this book, there will be no definitive answer given as to the use of one technology versus another technology, for this type of app versus that type of app. Also, do not forget that app development is a fast-paced, quickly changing world so what is suggested today may have moved on and changed in six months' time. The definitions of technically terminology such as Frameworks or native apps constantly change. Just as the definition of a phone, means something very different today that what it meant 50 years ago.

Finally, do not be put off by this chapter if you plan to be a C.E.O. or if you find yourself just on the business side of app development. This chapter is meant to give everyone involved in app development the fundamentals that will help them understand important development topics, such as which category of app should be developed and the development environment that should be used so the app is future-friendly.

The goal of this chapter is to present to you the different possibilities open to you and to discuss how they can be implemented, as well as to give you insight into both the development technologies that are currently available and the questions you need to ask yourself when developing an app. As the app developer, it is up to you to take the information provided here and apply it to the app you are developing.

The category of app and the technology used to produce the app are complex issues that must be carefully considered. There are many separate questions that must be combined for you to successfully produce an app.

In this chapter, we will break topics down into:

1. Type: The different *types* of apps that are available to develop
2. Technology: The different *development technologies* that exist, such as programming languages and different environments, and the SDKs and IDEs that are available

---

Goal of This Chapter

This chapter will help you understand the fundamentals of the technology that you can use to develop an app. By the end of the chapter you will understand how your different technology choices will affect the overall app.

Vocabulary Introduced

- App categories
  - Different types of apps that can be produced.
- Native apps
  - Apps that can be downloaded from an app store.
- Fully native apps
  - Apps that are developed using a first party IDE and downloaded from an app store.
- Hybrid apps
  - Apps that can be downloaded from an app store and then use a Chromeless browser to access a web page.
- Progressive Web Apps (PWA)
  - Web pages that have been specifically developed for mobile devices
- Programming languages
  - The various languages in which you can write code.
- Maturity
  - This refers to the how long a programming language has been widely used.
- Frameworks
  - A collection of software libraries grouped together.
- Integrated Development Environment (IDE)
  - A complete suite of tools to help you develop an app.
- Software Development Kit (SDK)
  - A framework with extra tools to help you develop an app.
- Code versioning
  - A system that helps either you or multiple people keep track of code (versions) as it is developed.

- Business as a Service (BaaS)
  - Companies that will provide the backend of technology such as servers for a fee.
- Device Features
  - This refers to technology within an mobile or technology device such as a camera.

Levels of Understanding

Below in Fig. 4.1 we see a breakdown of knowledge required to understand the basic requirements of the technology that affects apps.

- We see the core knowledge required which covers topics such as, what are the different types of apps, what are different programming languages and environments.
- Expanded Non-Technical in this area requires a deeper understanding of which type of type will suit the goals of your app?
- Expanded Technical knowledge required including a deeper understanding of topics such as what different technologies enable the app to achieve the goals of design and feature requirements.

Expanded Non-technical Understanding

1. What type of app best suits your needs?
2. Can non-tech give input into important development challenges e.g. The app must continue to work on old phones
3. Does non-tech have an understanding of technologies such as servers? and things that may need regular maintenance in the app?

Core Understanding
Types of apps
How will different designs affect the overall technical development of the app?
Realistic timelines/budget for different designs
Current best tools for creating a mock-up
Different types of development technology

Expanded Technical Understanding

1. Can you advise on the best
   - Type of app for the design given from Chp. III?
   - Which dev environment to use when programming the app?
   - Types of technologies required such as servers
   - How to develop the code for the lowest maintenance?
2. Does tech have a full understanding of mobile tech and how to utilize them to the app's advantage?
3. What is likely to change with mobile technology/programming languages that could affect the over all design of the app?

Fig. 4.1 Core, non-technical and technical understanding for this Chapter

Content

DISCLAIMER: All of the content in this chapter is meant as a guide. Exact uses and functionality of different forms of technologies such as third party IDE's changes rapidly. Therefore, please consult the manufacturers own documentation for correct, exact uses and functionality. The author of this book did not consult directly with any of manufacturers listed in this chapter.

Category of an App

There are many things that must be thought of before one line of code is written in the app development process. This chapter will break these ideas down for you so that you can make the right decision of which category of app is right for your project.

The category of app you will develop depends on a variety of factors:

- What is the app meant to do?
- Who is the target market?
- Does the app need to be updated often?
- Does the app have a lot of technology needs, such as access to hardware features or fast processing?
- How much money do you have for technical development?
- How long do you have for technical development?

As a technical app developer or the non-technical person in charge of getting an app made for your business/company/organization/music group etc., you must make a fundamental decision in the very beginning. This decision is not a simple one and can prove costly if you do not make the right one. You must have a core understanding of the category of apps available to develop.

What do we mean when we say category of app? Do you notice any difference from the apps on your mobile device? We do not mean the difference between a game app and a banking app, we mean the technology that is behind the app. The average person will never notice what category of app they have, but there is a big difference in how different types of apps are developed.

In this section, we will carefully break down the issues for you so that you will understand how to make the right decision when choosing between the different types of apps available.

In general, the category or type of app means:

- Native
- Hybrid
- Progressive Web App (PWA) (Fig. 4.2)

Understanding the difference between these different 'types' of apps will help you make the right decision about the category of app to develop in different scenarios. Of course, the fast -paced, changing world of app development can sometimes make it hard to make decisions on this is. D since decisions you make now could change or not be valid by next year.

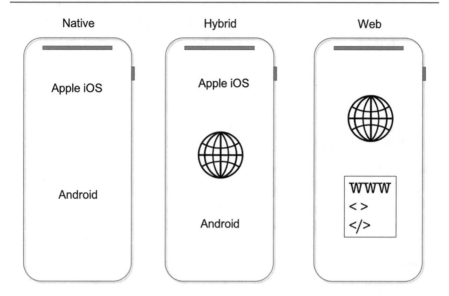

Fig. 4.2 The basic categories of Native, Hybrid and PWA apps

We will begin by examining these categories so that you understand what is meant by each term.

Exact categories for types of apps are becoming increasingly blurred. New technologies that increase the potential for cross -platform and hybrid and even PWA apps come out all the time.

For the purposes of this book, we will use this general classification:

1. Pure Native App – coded on manufacturer's IDE.
2. Cross-Platform Native App – coded using a third Party Framework that is then built to run natively on a manufacturer's device.
3. Hybrid App – coded to use a WebView with a wrapper that allows the app to be downloaded from a device manufacturer's app store and loaded directly onto a mobile device.
4. PWA – coded completely with web technologies and loaded from a website not an app store.

Native Apps

People will argue that any app that is installed on a mobile platform from an app store is a native app so that categories 1, 2 and 3 are all just native apps. But our intention is to teach you about the differences and not to argue exact classifications.

Native mobile apps are the most common type of app. Native apps are built for specific platforms, i.e. Apple or Android. You install native apps through a store, such as the App Store or the Google Play Store. Users access native apps through an icon on the home screen of their device.

Native apps have an intuitive interface. They naturally have the look and feel that users are used to. Native apps have full access to a device's features, such as:

- Camera
- User's list of contacts
- Accelerometer
- GPS
- Compass
- Multi-touch gestures

Native apps can be broken down into categories:

- **Fully Native** (sometimes known as Pure Native)
- **Native** (sometimes known as cross-platform native)
- **Natively Installed** (some people call any app available in an app store a natively installed app)

All types of native apps are available on the App Store or Google Play Store. All types of native apps are installed on the end user's device. All types of native apps are accessed by clicking an icon on the home screen. The difference is how they are coded, meaning which IDE/Framework was used to produce the app.

Fully Native Apps

Android Studio see https://developer. android.com/	Kotlin programming language see https://developer.android.com/kotlin	Java programming language see https://www.java.com/en/

Xcode see https://developer.apple. com/xcode/	Swift programming language see https://developer. apple.com/swift/

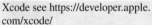

Fully Native apps (see Fig. 4.3: The different languages and IDEs/Frameworks that can be used to make a natively installed app) are developed in the device platform's IDE, i.e. Android Studio for Android or Xcode for Apple. Developing fully native apps means you get the support of the manufacturer of your intended device platform and that they will provide you with free development tools, documentation, etc. By developing a fully native app, you will always get access to the latest device features and manufacturer's programming libraries. Fully native apps are suited to apps that need the very best of everything: speed, device features,

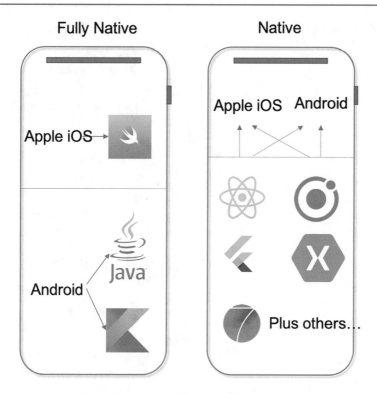

Fig. 4.3 The different languages and IDEs/Frameworks that can be used to make a natively installed app

manufacturer's libraries, etc. Examples of such apps might include a very technical, highly responsive augmented reality game or a sleek looking app.

Native - Third Party Frameworks

Third Party Frameworks are a cross -platform solution for native apps (Fig. 4.4: A selection of third Party frameworks for native app development). These frameworks make it possible to create a Native app without using the device manufacturer's IDE. This means you can code the app in a multitude of different languages, from C# to HTML. You can have one code base, and then compile the app to run on Apple or Android. Native third party framework apps have many of the benefits of fully native apps.

There are numerous third party frameworks to use to develop apps for Apple and Android. Three of the best known and used are:

- Flutter, supported by Google
- React Native, supported by Facebook
- Xamarin, supported by Microsoft

Fig. 4.4 A selection of
third Party frameworks for
native app development

Native App (Fully Native and Third Party Framework) – Pros

- Performance: Fully native apps and cross -platform native apps offer very good performance and run at a high speed. Native apps tend to work faster than web or hybrid apps. This may not be noticeable for a normal app, but it might be for a gaming app.
- Features: Native apps have full access to all the device features, such as push notifications and vibration.
- Offline: These apps can work offline. Functioning without the internet/cell data can be useful for various situations, such as in a power cut, on an airplane, etc. They are available through the App Store and the Google Play Store.
- UI/UX: Native apps have the look and feel that the end user will be used to.

Hybrid Apps

Hybrid apps are part Native and part Web app. Hybrid apps run in a simplified web browser, called a WebView. This is an app-embedded browser that links to a website. To achieve this, you need a native shell. This shell wraps around and loads the WebView object that runs the app. A WebView is known as a 'Chromeless Browser' because much of the normal browser is stripped away, such as the toolbar, URL address bar, etc. This can mean that the end user may not even be aware that they are running a WebView object. Hybrid apps have a lot of similarities to native apps. With new technologies coming out all the time, they are becoming more similar to native apps. The main difference between the two is the need to run the WebView and to connect to a website.

Similarities to fully native and third party native include:

- The app is installed through a store e., e.g. the App Store or the Google Play Store
- They can look just like native apps
- They can access device hardware like native apps

There are many frameworks designed to let you code a web app and then wrap it so that it becomes a hybrid/native app.

Hybrid Apps - Pros

- Cost: Hybrid Apps can offer a cost -sensitive solution to businesses on a budget. This is because the business will likely need a website and so the app will then simply load this website, thereby cutting down on development costs. The website that the WebView object is going to pull from must be coded as a responsive website (see Glossary). Having a responsive website may be more costly and burdensome than a standard website b, but it is very likely that, overall, it will be less costly and burdensome than a website plus an Apple and Android app. If your budget is limited and you want to have an app on the App Store, this may be the solution for you.
- Coding: You will only need one skill set to code in. To get the UI you want, you may have to code in some fully native languages, however this will be less time-consuming and less difficult than coding two distinct apps (Apple/Android).
- Time: Development time can be slower than compared to a fully native app because of developing one set of code.
- Maintenance: Maintenance or further development of the app is made easier because of a single code base.

In Fig. 4.5: A framework being used to stylise iOS, Android, you can see how hybrid builders are trying to imitate the look of the native mobile app. To do this, they rely on different frameworks.

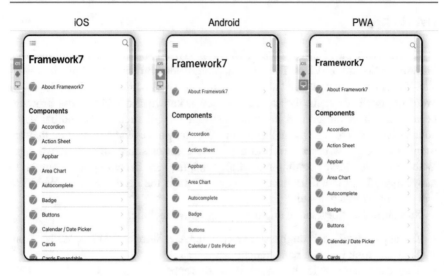

Fig. 4.5 A framework being used to stylise iOS, Android and PWA. (Source: https://framework7.io/)

Hybrid: Pros and Cons

- Cheaper to develop than native apps.
- One code set skill required (there may be a small amount of other language coding required).
- The coding language can be Web Technologies, such as HTML5, CSS, or JavaScript.
- You can also write in other programming languages.
- Development time is shorter.
- If you are developing a game or a very technical app, a hybrid app may not offer the performance that you are looking for.
- You will need to have the WebView object connect to a website and therefore internet connection is required.
- Hybrid apps may not offer the user the same experience end users are used to. Swipe gestures etc. may not respond the same as they do with a native app.

Progressive Web App (PWA)

PWA's are developed using web technologies (see Fig. 4.6: Web apps and the different technologies to code them in). These types of apps are basically web pages designed for mobile devices. They run in a normal web browser. Any platform that has a browser can run a PWA. It is basically an optimized website for mobile

Fig. 4.6 Web apps and the different technologies to code them in

devices. The users go to a URL of a website with a web browser and the website is coded in a way that it recognizes that the device connecting is a mobile device and not a desktop. The goal of a PWA is to not appear like a normal website on a mobile device. PWAs are coded to appear as much like a native app as they can, but the user interface and browser can make this difficult. PWAs cannot access all of a mobile device's features (but this is improving).

When developing any app, you must think about your end user (see Key Ingredient No. 1: The Four Ws). There are many reasons that a PWA may be advantageous for users. Maybe some of your end users have old devices. Lots of native apps cannot be downloaded onto old phones. What if your end user has an old phone? They would not be able to use lots of native apps, but they could use a PWA.

Discoverability: A PWA is not available in an app store. People access them by going to a website. Some say that not being in an app store is a positive aspect for PWAs discoverability because PWAs are searchable by a search engine. Others say that this factor is a negative for PWAs because end users often just search for apps in app stores. Once a user has found the PWA via a search engine, they can add an icon to the home screen. Then, to access it at a later time, they just tap the icon on their home screen like they would do with any native/hybrid app. The icon takes them directly to the correct website. However, it is not that easy for some users to add the icon to their home screen from a website. It is not even widely known that this functionality is possible.

Development: PWAs are built using web technologies such as HTML5, CSS3, and JavaScript. This means that people who code websites can develop mobile apps. However, there is no support from a device manufacturer for the look and feel of a native app nor support for access to device features. What if a device comes out with a button for fingerprint recognition and you want to utilize this feature? You will have to wait for web technologies to catch up or you simply won't be able to use the feature.

Data requirements: A PWA is generally much lighter in data requirements when compared to a native app.

Acceptance: Because PWAs are found not in an app store, you do not need to get the app accepted and you do not need to worry about making updates to your app (see Chap. 5: Trends/Digital Security/Compliance/Getting Accepted).

Twitter turned to a PWA [13]. It proved to be the perfect solution for some of Twitter's needs. Ultimately, Twitter went with a combination of a PWA and a hybrid for Android for Twitter Lite.

On May 10, 2019, it was reported that Tinder was planning for a lighter version app called Tinder Lite, aimed at growing markets where data usage, bandwidth and storage space are a concern [14].

PWAs – Pros and Cons

- If you create a PWA app, any device that can run a web browser will be able to run your app.
- PWAs are cheap to develop.
- PWAs can be released at any time, you can update whenever you want.
- PWAs do not need to be accepted by an app store.
- Updates are easy. The newest version always loads when a user opens a web app.
- Discoverability may be an issue.
- If the user does not download an icon to their device, you will be reliant on the user searching for the app in a search engine each time they want to use it. As a result, they may discover a similar app.

Choosing the Type of App

Here we provide a list of some of the factors to consider when making this decision. Perhaps the final decision will be a combination of categories/types of app.

Checklist

Non-Technical	Technical

Target market and end user
    What would suit them best?
Time to market
    Quick or not?
Budget
    Large or small?
UX/UI
    Sleek or basic? Touch gestures? Will the
    user interface change a lot?
Discoverability
    Will users search for your app or go to a
    store?
Updates
    How often will you update the app?
	Device capabilities requirements
	    Does your app have a lot of technical
	    requirements, lots of processing power, lots
	    of touch gestures, etc.
	Offline requirements
	    Do you want parts of the app to function
	    without the internet?
	App's responsiveness
	    Is the app a fast -paced, very graphical
	    game?
	Skillset required
	    Which IDE and programming language best
	    suits the non-technical requirements?
	Future -friendly
	    IDE/programming language
	Updates
	    How often will you update the app?
	Data requirements
	    Where is the data for the app coming from,
	    e.g. servers constantly updating
	    information?

*Maintenance, along with many other categories, can be argued one way or another. Different app requirement scenarios will give you different outcomes as to whether Native/Hybrid or PWA would be easier or harder to maintain. If the device manufacturer brings out a new feature, such as Apple did in the UI for iOS 7, fully native allows you to simply recompile your code and the update is done. For other types of apps, you may have to do a substantial amount of coding to make the UI look like what would have been provided with Xcode. However, if data that feeds the UI needs updating, you can quickly do this with a PWA without any need to do an update through the App Store. So, in this scenario, a PWA would win the maintenance ease-of-use war. For this reason, we have tried to give you a general overview in the comparison charts; however, with all of the categories you must look at different scenarios and what suits each scenario (Figs. 4.7, 4.8, 4.9, and 4.10).

TYPE	App Stores	Google Search	Wrapper	Multiple Languages	Quick Deployment	Cheap
Pure Native	✓	✗	✗	✓	✗	✗
Native Cross Platform	✓	✗	✗	✗	✓	✓
Hybrid	✓	✗	✓	Maybe	✓	✓
PWA	✗	✓	✗	✗	✓	✓

Fig. 4.7 Shows Native to PWA compatibility with various topics

TYPE	UI/UX	Performance	Support	Future Forward	Support for very old devices
Pure Native	✓+++	✓+++	✓+++	✓+++	✗
Native Cross Platform	✓++	✓+++	✓++	✓++	✗
Hybrid	✓+	✓++	✓	✓++	✓
PWA	✓	✓	✗	✓+++	✓+++

Fig. 4.8 Shows Native to PWA compatibility with various topics

	Native	Hybrid	PWA
Different Languages	Yes	Maybe	No
Development Time	Long	Medium	Short
Development Costs	High	Medium	Low
Support from IDE	High	High/Medium	N/A
Performance Speed	High	High/Medium	Dependent on factors
Device Access	High	High	Improving
UX/UI	High	High/Medium	Improving
UX/UI	Provided	High/Medium	Bespoke
Offline	Yes	Yes	Some
Time to market	Long	Medium	Short
Access to App Stores	Yes	Yes	No
Maintenance	Depends*	Depends*	Depends*

Fig. 4.9 Shows Native to PWA compatibility with various topics

	Native	Hybrid	PWA
Cross Platform	No	Yes	Yes
Discoverability	App Stores	App Stores	Search Engine
Update difficulty	High	Medium	Low
Sleek design look	Yes	Yes	Improving
Feature Access	High	High	Medium

Fig. 4.10 App dev

Development Technology

Once you have decided on the category of app you plan to develop, you will need to pick a programming language and a development programming environment. Both of these decisions come fall under the umbrella term of *development technology*. What technology you use to develop your app requires lots of thought.

- How will you code your app?
- How will it be developed?
- What language will you use?
- Which programming environment will you use?

In this section, we will give a brief introduction to some of the languages and environments involved with developing apps. This will give you a foundation for understanding the complexities of choosing the right development technology (Fig. 4.11).

In picking which programming language and environment to use, you will need to make decisions such as:

- What are the project's goals regarding the technology aspect?
- Which development programming languages are going up in trend?
- Which development programming languages/environments have been around for a long time?
- Which development programming languages/environments are right for the type of app I am developing
- What are the target devices for the app?
- Which platforms do the target devices run on?
- What skillset does your team have?
- If you do not have a team, how easy is it to get a team in the language development environment that you choose?

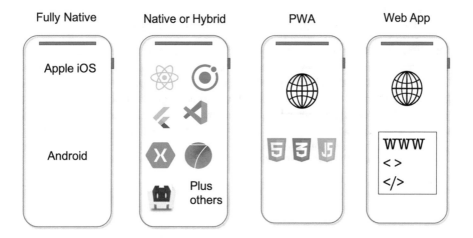

Fig. 4.11 Showing fully native all the way to web app

- How many technical development people will you need to be able to make the app in the language and programming environment that you have chosen?
- How much development time do you have?
- When do you plan to do the first release of your app?
- How much maintenance and future development do you envision?
- Are your technical decisions going to be future-friendly?

Here we are going to take you through some technology tools you will need to develop your app. We will break them down into two main categories:

- Development Environments
- Programming Languages

The decision you make in the following two sections should come after you have made a decision about the category or type of app you are going to develop.

Development Environments

A development environment is the program that lets you write the code that will become your app. Development environments come in a variety of different formats from fully fledged Integrated Development Environments (IDE) to code text editors. Here is a basic list of terms used for a development environment:

- Integrated Development Environments (IDE)
  - This is a complete environment that includes an SDK.
- Software Development Kit (SDK)
  - This has everything you need to develop software, but it may be missing some extra features that make developing software easier.
- Frameworks or Libraries
  - These are software frameworks or libraries that you can use to write code
- Code Editor
  - This is a basic code editor. It will be lighter in data terms.

The difference between different types of development environments can be blurry. A development environment will let you or a programmer write text (code) in a certain way that can then be turned into an app. The development environment will help with integrated features such as automated code generation, the same as text prediction in messaging apps and other features like compilation and a graphical user interface (GUI), all designed to help the programmer code the program.

How much the development environment does for you depends on the one that you choose to use. Here we will talk about some of the most well-known development environments (Fig. 4.12).

Fig. 4.12 Xcode interface

Xcode - IDE   https://developer.apple.com/Xcode/

Xcode is Apple's IDE and was developed for creating iOS apps. At the time of publication, the current version is Xcode 12.5. You can run Xcode on any MacOS system. You will need to update Xcode approximately once a month. Updates take at least 1 hour.

Apple provides the WWDC – Worldwide developer conference once a year [15]. The WWDC provides tutorials on programming techniques/design philosophies, competitions and everything else you need to know to be an amazing tech developer.

Android Studio IDE   https://developer.android.com/studio

Android studio is the official IDE for Google's Android's operating system. At the time of publication, the current version is 4.1.3. You can run android studio on windows, macOS, Linux, chrome OS.

Listed below are some of the most well-known third party IDE's, SDK's or development environments. Please consult the manufacturers website for exact uses and functionality Fig. 4.13.

Apache Cordova
Mobile apps with HTML, CSS and JS

Xamarin by
Microsoft
Develop using visual studio
Create native apps

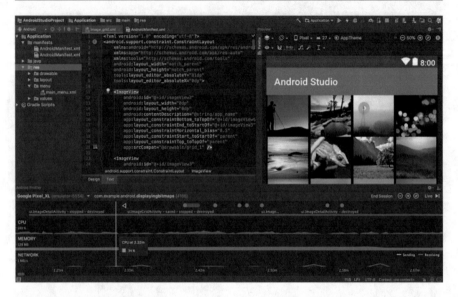

Fig. 4.13 Android Studio interface

Flutter by Google Designed to work with iOS and android plus web complies with machine code.	No wrapper, partly complies with Native Code (UI) then runs virtual machine in background Language: JavaScript	Adds wrapper to your Web app Language: JavaScript
React native By Facebook Partly complies With native code. Comes with some native UI Components	Vue JavaScript framework	Angular maintained by Google Type script language for PWAs or native apps

React/React Native

These are frameworks designed for making mobile apps. Facebook developed React as an alternative to the standard MVC frameworks that were available at the time. React, (also written as ReactJS or React.js) is a JavaScript library that was developed to build user interfaces. Also developed and maintained by Facebook, React Native is an extension of React. React and React Native do not come with an IDE, but you can use them in Visual Studio Code.

React Native was released in 2015 for native mobile software development. It too is written with JavaScript, a well-known programming language, and it for use of native mobile functionalities and integration.

> React Native is an open-source mobile application framework created by Facebook, Inc. It is used to develop applications for Android, Android TV, iOS, macOS, tvOS, Web, Windows and UWP by enabling developers to use React's framework along with native platform capabilities [16].

Checklist Development Environment

- Can be used make the category/type of app that is required
- Skill set/team can use this development environment
- Will be future-friendly

Environment	Native	Popular	Wrapper	Language	Native Components	Cross-Platform	Access Device
Android Studio	Yes	High +++	No	Java/Kotlin	Yes	No	Total
Xcode	Yes	High +++	No	Swift	Yes	No	Total
	Yes	High ++	No	Javascript	Some	Yes	Good+
Flutter	Yes	High	No	Dart	UI tool for native components	Yes	Good++
IONIC	Yes	Middle	Yes	Javascript	Adaptive	Yes	Good
	Yes	Middle	Yes	C#	Yes	Yes	Good++

Environment	Native	Popular	Wrapper	Language	Native Components	Cross-Platform	Access Device
	Yes	Lower	No	Javascript	Some	Almost	Good++
	Yes	Middle	Yes	Web technologies	No	Yes	Lower
Web	No	High+++	No	Web technologies	No	Yes	Lower

Programming Languages

Combined with the decision of which programming environment to use is the decision of which programming language to use.

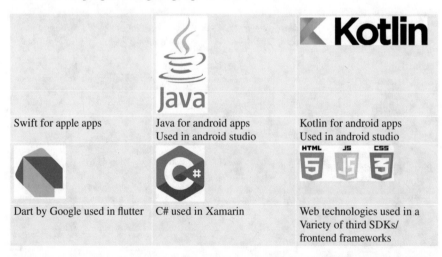

Swift for apple apps	Java for android apps Used in android studio	Kotlin for android apps Used in android studio
Dart by Google used in flutter	C# used in Xamarin	Web technologies used in a Variety of third SDKs/ frontend frameworks

Swift   https://developer.apple.com/swift/

Swift is the programming language used by apple. You code in swift inside of Xcode.
// how to write 'hello world' in swift
Print("hello world! I am beginning app dev!!!")

Java   https://www.java.com/en/

Java is a high-level, class-based, object-oriented programming language. It is a general-purpose programming language intended to let application developers *write once, run anywhere* (WORA).
// how to write 'hello world' in swift
System.Out.Println("hello world! I am beginning app dev!!!");

Kotlin   https://developer.android.com/kotlin

In 2019, Google announced that Kotlin would be the preferred language for Android development. Kotlin is designed to interoperate fully with Java.
// How to write 'hello world' in Kotlin
println("Hello World! I am beginning App Dev!!!")

Dart   https://dart.dev/

A programming language developed by Google that is optimized for UI development.
// How to write 'hello world' in Dart
print('Hello World! I am beginning App Dev!!!');

JavaScript   https://www.javascript.com/

JavaScript is considered a core technology of the world wide web
// How to write 'hello world' in JavaScript
alert("Hello World! I am beginning App Dev!!!");

C#   https://docs.microsoft.com/en-us/dotnet/csharp/

C# is a general-purpose, component-orientated programming language developed by Microsoft.
// How to write 'hello world' in JavaScript
Console.WriteLine("Hello World! I am beginning App Dev!!!");

Here is a list of things you may want to consider when choosing which programming language you will use to develop your app. This decision will also be tied to which programming environment you choose.

- How new is the language?
- How much is it being used?
- Is it likely to increase in use or decrease in use/popularity?
- Is there a lot of talent that can code in the language?
- If your programming team changed, could new coders easily adapt to the language you choose?

Language	Cross-Platform	Popularity	Mature	Talent available	Environments
Java	Yes	High +++	Yes +++	High	Android Studio
Swift	No	High +++	Yes	Yes, but expensive	Xcode
JavaScript	Yes	High ++	No	High	
Dart	Yes	High	No	Less	
C#	Yes	Middle	Yes	Less	
Web technologies	Yes	Middle	Yes +++	High	

Code Versioning Tools

Developing software is an on-going project. There will be many versions of your app. There may be multiple people working on it. How will you make sure that you have the latest version of code? How will you go back if you discover a bug? It is possible to email different versions to team members, however this is not the best solution and is likely to cause many problems. The solution is for your team to use code versioning tools. Examples of code versioning tools are: Git, Mercurial or SVN.

Development Technology Checklist

Use the below list to help you decide on the technology requirements for your project.

- Language?
- Team skills?
- Cost of new developers?
- Maturity of language?
- Trend of use?
- Maturity of IDE/Code Editor/Languages?
- Team skills?
- New team members?

Decision
- Category/Type of app
- Development environment
- Programming language

Technology – BaaS

It is very likely that your app cannot stand alone. It is likely to require things such as data storage, notifications, cloud infrastructure. This is known as the backend of an app. You can get all the services you will require from large reputable companies such as Google, AWS, IBM and Microsoft. This is known as BaaS – Backend as a Service. No two providers offer exactly the same services and what they do provide changes all the time so you will need to do some investigation.

BaaS services can provide everything from AI services to Databases to Blockchain capabilities and more. These services are typically provided on a pay-as-you-go charging model, which is great for you as a new app developer. This provides you with multiple benefits: you do not need a large upfront investment to get your app going, you do not need to worry about maintaining software and the security of things (such as databases) and, if your app proves popular and gets lots and lots of end users, you can automatically scale without any issues.

These cloud/BaaS companies can help with everything from:

- Back end servers
- Databases
- Real-time Data
- Hosting
- Storage
- Scaling – to more users
- Authentication
- Notifications
- Cloud messaging
- App indexing

- Advertising sales
- Crash testing and analytics

Here is a list of the most well-known companies:

Firebase by Google
     https://firebase.google.com/
Amazon web Services
     https://aws.amazon.com/
Microsoft azure
     https://azure.microsoft.com/
IBM
     https://www.ibm.com/services

Chapter Summary

There are many factors to consider when choosing between a Native, Hybrid or PWA app. There is no right or wrong answer, and no steadfast rules for choosing the category of app that you develop. The choices all depend on the project. The solution may be a combination of various types of apps.

You must take all the factors you have learnt in this chapter into consideration and then apply them to your project.

Further Reading

To learn more about these topics do internet searches for reputable and up-to-date videos and documentation on the following topics:

- Native vs Hybrid vs Web apps
- How to create mobile apps
- Third Party IDE's, SDK's, Frameworks for mobile app development
- Third Party Frameworks comparisons
- Choosing a mobile app framework
- Using BaaS
- BaaS providers

Case Studies

Exercises

Exercise No. 13
These are some example scenarios. Fill in some basic ideas on the requirements for the following apps.

- Gaming App
- Shopping App

- Newspaper App
- Insurance Company App with reporting accident functionality
- Emergency Alert Information App
- COVID Tracking App
- Your own idea

App	End User	UI/UX	Discoverability	Internet requirements	Device features
Gaming					
Shopping					
News					
Insurance					
Emergency alert					
COVID tracking					
Your own idea					

Which type of app (Native, Hybrid, PWA, Combination) would you choose for the following applications? List them below.

- Gaming app
- Shopping app
- Newspaper app
- Insurance company app with reporting accident functionality
- Emergency alert information app
- COVID green pass app
- Your own idea

Exercise No. 14
Can you think of a way to have a native app whose data changes constantly without the need to update the app constantly?

Exercise No. 15
- Find five apps that are fully native and coded in either Swift or Java/Kotlin.
- Find five hybrid apps. List the language and IDE used to develop the app.
- Find five apps that are progressive web apps or simple web apps.
- What languages are used for native apps?
- What languages are used for progressive web apps?
- What languages are used for hybrid apps?

Individual Reflection

To solidify your understanding in 500 words write out what you have learnt from this chapter. Here are some hints that you might use to write about.

- What is the difference between; Native, Hybrid and PWA apps?
- Suggest a reason to use each of the above types of apps.
- What programming languages are mature and which are the latest programming languages?

Knowledge Check

Fill in the blanks of the following sentence:

Use the words provided in the word bank.

*Apps that are coded in a platforms IDE (such as ....
or ....) plus they are also coded in their own language (such
as .... Or ....) are known
as .... apps. Apps that are developed in a generic IDE are
known as .... apps. A .... app is a website that has
been coded specifically for mobile devices. Using services from another company
such as server storage or user authentication is known as ....*

Word Bank:

Xcode, Android Studio, Swift, Javascript, Java, Kotlin, Cross Native, Fully
Native, BaaS, PWA, IDE, SDK,

Answers

Below are suggested answers to the exercise given in this chapter. They are not
complete and simply a suggestion to help you further think about your own solutions. You may well come up with a different or better solution. This is part of the
app development process.

Exercise No. 13

These are some scenarios. Fill in some basic ideas on the requirements for the following apps.

- Gaming App
- Shopping App
- Newspaper App
- Insurance Company App with reporting accident functionality
- Emergency Alert Information App
- COVID Tracking App

App	End User	UI/UX	Discoverability	Internet requirements	Device features
Gaming	Approx. Age 18 to 60. Over 50% male	Very slick High quality graphics	Internet & app stores	Requires high speed internet	Microphone, contacts Geo data for local teams
Shopping	All ages and genders	Lead people to pay button Broken in categories	Internet & app stores	No special requirements. However, slow internet speed might cause low latency	Digital wallet, Camera for possible virtual try on of clothes, tracking of personal choices for ads

App	End User	UI/UX	Discoverability	Internet requirements	Device features
News	Typically over 18	Easy to read	Internet & app stores		Geo data for local news
Car insurance	Over age to legally drive in country provided	Simple, navigation steps required for a task should be kept to a minimum	Internet & app stores		Camera
Emergency alert			App stores for notifications		GPS, notifications
COVID green pass			App stores		Bluetooth for alerting of people close by

Which type of app (Native, Hybrid, PWA, Combination) would you choose for the following applications? List them below.
- Gaming app
  - Native needs high performance
- Shopping app
  - Hybrid/PWA, will be updated a lot
- Newspaper app: Hybrid/PWA will be updated a lot
  - Hybrid with good native experience
- Insurance company app with reporting accident functionality
  - Possibility just PWA needs to be easily discovered by a google search
- Emergency alert information app
  - Hybrid should be very platform independent, UI is not so important
- COVID green pass app
  - Hybrid should be very platform independent, UI is not so important. Some components will need to be downloaded with the app in case internet is not available when being used.

Exercise No. 14

Can you think of a way to have a native app whose data changes constantly without the need to update the app constantly?
- At Citizen Alert Inc. to overcome this problem we came up with the following solution, which will not be completely disclosed here due to company intellectual protection. The basis was to have a completely native app that pulled data from a database as it loaded. The system developed was not that simple but hopefully it will give you something to think about.

Exercise No. 15

• What apps did you find?
• Is it possible to discover if an app is hybrid?

Knowledge Check Answer

*Apps that are coded in a platforms IDE (such as **Android Studio** or **Xcode**) plus they are also coded in their own language (such as **Kotlin** Or **Swift**) are known as **Fully Native** apps. Apps that are developed in a generic IDE are known as **Cross Native** apps. A **PWA** app is a website that has been coded specifically for mobile devices. Using services from another company such as server storage or user authentication is known as **BaaS**.*

Case Studies

Here, we will look at real life examples and what decisions were taken into account on the category of app to be developed.

Citizen Alert App (Fig. 4.14)

When making the decision for how Citizen Alert's apps would be developed, the company opted for Fully Native.

Why? Citizen Alert makes apps for small towns to communicate with their citizens. Sometimes, this means emergency communications. As a result, the company decided that push notifications were absolutely essential and having the apps function without any failures was critical. Also the company wanted to develop apps that portrayed a level of excellence in areas such as UI/UX and so it was felt that fully native could provide this.

An additional reason was that the programming team already had the skillset of the Swift and Java Programming Languages. They were developing a white label app (see Glossary). This meant that once the initial development was over, updating would be relatively easy. Things can change a lot with Apple and they wanted to have the security of using Apple's IDE.

Citizen Info App (Fig. 4.15)

Citizen Info is an app developed by Citizen Alert Inc. The idea behind the app is to provide up -to -date information on large cities in North America. The idea came from a high number of requests for such an app from end users. End users were seeing the company name (Citizen Alert Inc.) and presuming that they could get info on their city. So, Citizen Alert decided to develop such an app for a general audience in North America.

This app is ideal for a Hybrid or a PWA app. Why? The data changes rapidly in this app and always needs to be up-to-date and there are no notifications. A Choosing

Fig. 4.14 Citizen Alert a
white label app

Fig. 4.15 Citizen Info app

a native app would have meant updating the app constantly. Therefore, and therefore a native app would normally be out of the question, but the app was an offshoot of the Citizen Alert app that the company already had, meaning the code base could be reused to make Citizen Info. What was solution did the company picked? We shall put the answer in the answers section of this book.

In the Compliance section (see Chap. 5: Trends/Digital Security/Compliance/ Getting Accepted we will discuss why this app was removed from the App store by Apple once and removed from the Google Play Store twice, before ultimately being removed completely by the Google Play Store. In the App Economics section (see Chap. 6: *Monetization*), we will discuss why this app was banned from Google Ads for one month and the different solutions the company used to overcome the issue with Google Ads.

Trends/Digital Security/Compliance/ Getting Accepted

5

Special Note*: At the time of the first edition of this book being completed, beginning of March 2022, war has broken out between Ukraine and Russia. This has heightened the concern of Cyberwarfare. Cyberwarfare is the use of digital attacks against a perceived enemy state or enemy country. It is believed that using cyberwarfare could have the potential to cause similar harm to physical warfare [17]. This has only made digital security more essential and vital. If you are developing an app please expand your knowledge of the topic outside of what can be covered in this book.*

This chapter aims to teach you about 'future thinking' or keeping up with various trends within the app development world. It also aims to give insight into making sure that your app is accepted on the app stores and into understanding how your app must adhere to various compliance rules, Finally, we will look at security issues.

In this chapter, we will cover the following topics:

- Trends (Networks sand storage/Hardware/Mobile devices/Software)
- App store acceptance
- Compliance
- Digital Security

Goal of This Chapter

The aim of this chapter is to help you understand the fundamentals of technology trends and how this will topic will need to be something that you consider in any app development. We also introduce topics such as, compliance that must be addressed to get an app on any app store. This chapter also touches on the complex topic of data protection, security and vulnerabilities.

© The Author(s), under exclusive license to Springer Nature Switzerland AG 2022   113
T. Salter, *Technological and Business Fundamentals for Mobile App Development*, https://doi.org/10.1007/978-3-031-13855-3_5

Vocabulary Introduced

- Trends
  - This refers to the trends that are occurring in any domain of technology such as screen sizes.
- Internet of Things (IoT)
  - The IoT is all technology devices that are connected to the internet. This could be a door bell or a car.
- Cloud computing
  - On demand computer system resources that are provided over the internet.
- Compliance
  - Terms and conditions that you must adhere to get your app on an app store.
- Acceptance
  - The process you must go through to your app on an app store.
- Digital security
  - Protecting data and other things such as access to systems from vulnerabilities.
- Data protection
  - Protecting data that is either stored on a device/server or is travelling over a network.
- Vulnerabilities
  - These are the points of weakness that could be attacked by a malign actor.
- Data at rest
  - Digital data that is stored on any device
- Data in motion
  - Digital data that is moving over any type of network
- Malware
  - Malicious software that is intent of doing some form of harm.
- Enterprise data
  - Data that belongs to a company rather than an individual.
- Authentication
  - Confirming a user's identity.

Levels of Understanding

Below in Fig. 5.1 we see a breakdown of knowledge required to understand trends in the app development world. Plus the knowledge you will need to ensure that your app is compliant.

- We see the core knowledge required which covers topics such as compliance issues, getting an app accepted onto different app stores..
- Expanded Non-Technical in this area requires a deeper understanding of ethics and legal requirements found in app development.

Expanded Non-technical Understanding

1. What will the current target market and end user being using in the future? Will the app need to be adapted?
2. How likely is the end user to be doing everything in the cloud?
3. Are there non-technical compliance issues that the technical side must be made aware of such as ethics, legal?
4. Can they inform tech of domain requirements such as Canadian data storage rules

Core Understanding
What is a mobile device?
(laptops/smart phones/tablets/in home devices/wearable devices)
Future Trends
What is the IoT?
Cloud Computing
Compliance issues for iOS/Android
Case studies of compliance issues for well-known apps
Future Challenges
How has COVID affected mobile computing?
Investigate network tech & services
Look at different tech outside of mobile devices
Look at tech in mobile devices.

Expanded Technical Understanding

1. What a the major compliance issues on the technical side such as OS compatibility, changes in the way apps will be developed in the near future?

Fig. 5.1 Core, Non-Technical and Technical understanding for this Chapter

- Expanded Technical knowledge required including a deeper understanding of topics such as having enough technical understanding to make sure that an app fulfils compliance issues.

Content

Trends

Trends are very important in mobile app development. There are lots of different trends, such as:

- UI/UX trends
- Gesture trends
- Software development trends
- Hardware trends, for example smaller or bigger phones
- Internal technology trends, such as Bluetooth, Near Field Communication (NFC), and network trends.

You must keep ahead of trends and try to predict which way things are progressing in order to keep your app development relevant. If your competitors keep up on trends and their app can do something that your app cannot, you may lose out.

You must consider all of the above trends when developing an app. You can ask yourself questions such as:

- What will your current target market and end user be using for a device in the future?
- Will the app need to be adapted to new technologies?
- Think about what screens will your user have? OLED and E-ink in one device?
- Will keyboards exit? They are still here, but will they be taken over by touch screens – voice controlled – mind controlled? Will keyboards become projected or will they disappear to voice technology?
- What will mobile phones be like in 2 years? Foldable/stretchable phones? How often are voice calls made now?
- How will your end user be signing in – fingerprint/retina scan?

Think about these things and more in the beginning so that you can have a road map to the future.

Hardware

The lines between different hardware technologies are becoming increasingly blurred. It can now be hard to distinguish a clear line for describing what is a computer vs. what is a cellular phone.

Always think about future hardware trends in technology. It may take a year of development before your app is in the app stores. Think about how much mobile phones have changed in the last 5 years. Now you can understand that if you spent one year working on an app and you didn't keep up with hardware trends, your app may be out -of -date as soon as it is launched. To give a name to the ever expanding hardware technology market, it is termed the Internet of Things (IoT). Your app may have to connect with a plethora of different devices.

When you are in the beginning stages of developing your app, you must start to think beyond just designing or developing for current phones or tablets. Try to think about new technology that is coming up, such as different types of phones or other devices. Smart watches are becoming increasingly popular, so you may need to consider whether your app will need to function on some sort of wearable computing device. The wearable technology market is ever expanding. Will your app need to be compatible with this market?

With the change in work environments due to COVID-19, many office employees now work from home or their local coffee shop. Lots of people are now what is termed a digital nomad, this is a person who can work from anywhere. This means that increasingly what was considered office software will need to function on mobile devices, such as laptops and mobile phones or other mobile devices such as watches.

How many homes are now smart homes? What about in 5 years? Maybe your app will need to communicate with a smart home device? For example, think about an app for home security and think of all the devices that this type of app may need to connect with: doorbells, water sensors, door sensors, stove sensors, and the list goes on and on. Some of this can be viewed as simple data transfer over a Wireless or Bluetooth network y. You may not need to consider it in your app development, but it should be something you are aware of. Your app may need to connect via Bluetooth to a fridge or even to a toilet. Connected toilets are already here. The idea is that an elderly person can have a technology connected toilet in their home. The toilet can do some simple analysis of samples and contact the doctor if necessary or even give recipe suggestions. Perhaps your app will need to run on some sort of home security hub? A home security hub may have a different operating system from Android or Apple.

What devices should a health app consider?

- A watch
- A bed
- A toilet

What devices should an insurance app consider?

- In car technology
- A watch

Mobile Devices

The mobile devices that we use change at a very fast pace. First, cellular phones got smaller. Then, they got bigger to become so-called phablets (phone/tablet). Try to keep abreast of how the mobile device market is trending. Will there even be 'smartphones' in the future?

It is your job as a developer to keep track of trends. In 2013, LG, a large South Korean company, was the world's third-largest phone manufacturer. After a series of losses and phones that did not catch on, such as the Banana phone (a curved phone), it decided to leave the smartphone market. In April 2021, it announced that it was stopping its manufacturing of smartphones [18].

Just recently, flip phones were considered an out-of-date piece of technology. They were relegated to being solely for the elderly. That was until, after some not-so-successful flip phones, Samsung revived the market with the Galaxy Z Flip3 (Figs. 5.2 and 5.3).

Software Development

Software development for apps also changes at a rapid pace. Within six months to a year, there will be different software libraries, updated IDEs, and new ways of doing things. This, again, is something that you will need to keep abreast of.

Fig. 5.2 An older flip phone. (Source: https://images.macrumors.com/t/YV87b0F1cRKBujKBKOkQc7hhF6Y=/1600x900/smart/article-new/2019/09/samsung-flip-phone.jpg)

Fig. 5.3 The newly designed Samsung flip phone. (Source: https://www.theguardian.com/technology/2020/feb/19/samsung-galaxy-z-flip-review-back-to-the-folding-flip-phone-future)

Networks and Storage

How likely is the end user to be doing everything in the cloud? Will devices of the future have any data storage on them? What if you are developing a video or photo app -- will this affect how you develop it?

Acceptance and Compliance

Once you have developed your app, getting it accepted by the app stores is not guaranteed. This book has divided this topic into two sections:

1. Compliance
2. Acceptance

Whilst every app is similar and there are some overlaps, the topics are distinct enough to warrant being separated.

Compliance

Compliance issues for iOS/Android are a very important and complex issue that you must consider very early on. Compliance is a word you need to fully understand. It can take a lot of time and money to develop an app and there is a chance that you could spend a lot of time and money only to have your app refused by the app stores. You do not simply submit an app to the App Store and Google Play Store and they get accepted. When you first have an idea for an app or are asked to develop an app, you must check whether the app passes both Apple and Google's compliance rules. Compliance rules change all the time. What is compliant today may not be so tomorrow. COVID-19 and misinformation have recently changed a lot of compliance rules.

There may be non-technical compliance issues that the technical side must be made aware of such as ethics and legal issues.

Case Studies

Parler App (Fig. 5.4)

In 2018, two Computer Science alumni from University of Denver founded Parler, a free speech social media platform. By May 2019, Parler had 100,000 users [19].

COVID-19 changed the world in many ways, one of which was the idea that social media companies began policing what people were writing or posting about on their platforms. Many saw Parler as an alternative to Twitter, which had begun flagging prominent people's tweets as "misinformation." The Parler app was reportedly downloaded almost a million times in the week following the USA Election

Fig. 5.4 Picture of the Parler App

Day on November 3, 2020, and it rose to the top of both the Apple and Google Play Store's lists of the most popular free apps [19].

Following the events of January 6, 2021, Parler received a lot of push back from big tech companies.

- January 8, 2021: Google announced it was pulling Parler from its Google Play Store citing Parler's lack of "moderation policies and enforcement" that posed a "public safety threat" [20].
- January 9, 2021: Apple pulled Parler from its App Store. Although it was reported that Tim Cook was looking at ways to bring Parler back to the App Store [21]
- January 9, 2021: Amazon pulled Parler from its Amazon Web Services.

Other tech companies that stopped doing business with Parler included Twilio, which Parler used for two-factor authentication, and ScyllaDB, which Parler used for database services [22].

I Am Rich App (Fig. 5.5)

Developed by Armin Heinrich, the "I Am Rich" app sold for $999.99 on the App Store in 2008, which was the advent of the App Store. This was the maximum any app could be sold for on the App Store.

What did the app do? When you downloaded the app, you got an icon on your home screen of a red circle/gem and when you opened the app you had the same red circle/gem with an information button. If you clicked the information button there was a pop-up that read "I am rich I deserv it I am good, healthy & successful"... Yes, as you probably noticed, the word "deserve" was spelled incorrectly. Eight people purchased the app before Apple pulled it [23]. "I have no idea why they did it and am not aware of any violation of the rules to sell software on the App Store," Heinrich said in an e-mail with The Times today [24].

Fig. 5.5 Screenshot of original Apple Store page

Armin Heinrich

I Am Rich

Category: Lifestyle
Released Aug 05, 2008
Seller: Armin Heinrich
© 2008 Armin Heinrich
Version: 1.0
0.1 MB

$999.99   BUY APP

Fig. 5.6 Citizen Info app

Citizen Info App (Fig. 5.6)

Citizen Info/Alert App was an app developed by Citizen Alert Inc. after demand from end users. Citizen Alert Inc. develops communications apps for small towns but, after they received an unprecedented number of requests for information about cities in North America, they decided to act quickly and produced the app we see here (Fig. 5.7).

The *'Citizen Info/Alert App'* was pulled from Google Play Store. The issues were that the app linked to various government websites. Google Play said that Citizen Alert Inc. was making misleading claims by pretending to be endorsed by government agencies. As a company, we thought we were providing a great free service for citizens. We tried as many ways as we could think of such as adding pop-ups saying" we have no connection to the government agency, etc.". However, the attempts were in vain and the app is not available on the Google Play Store anymore. Below are some of the real emails received by Citizen Alert Inc. about the Alert App (Figs. 5.8, 5.9, and 5.10)

Governments

Even governments can face compliance issues. In the United Kingdom, the countries of England and Wales had a contact tracing app on both the Google Play Store

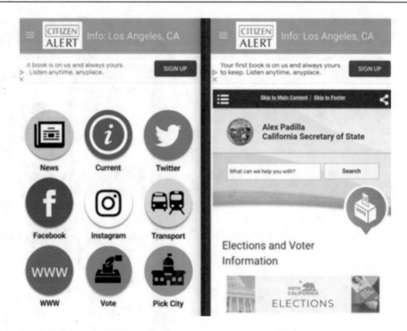

Fig. 5.7 Linking to Government Websites

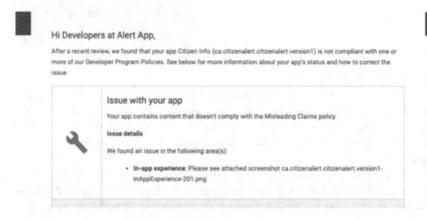

Fig. 5.8 Email from Google

and the App Store for COVID-19 contact tracing. As both England and Wales were going to be easing COVID restrictions and opening up social venues such as pubs, they attempted to update their contact tracing app to include the ability for users to upload logs of venue check-ins (location data) via a QR scan code (see Fig. 5.11: Screenshot of the NHS app and Fig. 5.12: NHS app). The update was blocked by both Google and Apple. Each company cited that the update violated agreed-upon terms for contact tracing apps.

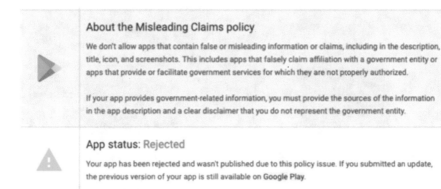

About the Misleading Claims policy

We don't allow apps that contain false or misleading information or claims, including in the description, title, icon, and screenshots. This includes apps that falsely claim affiliation with a government entity or apps that provide or facilitate government services for which they are not properly authorized.

If your app provides government-related information, you must provide the sources of the information in the app description and a clear disclaimer that you do not represent the government entity.

App status: Rejected

Your app has been rejected and wasn't published due to this policy issue. If you submitted an update, the previous version of your app is still available on Google Play.

Fig. 5.9 Email from Google

Action required: Submit an updated app for review

Here's what to do to help get your app on Google Play:

1. Read through the Misleading Claims policy and this Play Console Help Center article for more details. Learn more about privacy policy requirements on the Personal and Sensitive Information policy page.

2. Visit Google Play's Academy for App Success to get contextual learning on Google Play policy.

3. Make appropriate changes to your app, and be sure to address the issue described above. Also check your app's store listing for compliance, if applicable.

4. Double check that your app is compliant with all other Developer Program Policies.

5. Sign in to your Play Console and submit the update to your app.

Contact support

Fig. 5.10 Email from Google

Governments

Fig. 5.11 Screenshot of the NHS app

Fig. 5.12 NHS app

In the terms of both Apple's and Google's privacy agreement for contact-tracing tech, the apps were not allowed to collect any location data. Therefore, both stores rejected the new update put forward by the Department of Health for each of the countries [25].

Acceptance

Acceptance by the App Store and the Google Play Store is becoming increasingly difficult. The rules on acceptance are becoming stricter and even just having an idea for which there are already lots of existing apps can get your app rejected. You can be rejected for many different reasons, including everything from design guidelines to political reasons. Apple will even reject your app if they are going to make this type of app in the future [26].

There are things you need to think about to ensure that your app will be accepted on the Google Play Store and App Store. Both stores have many acceptance rules and regulations. This can be a decision that must be juggled between when to release your app vs. how much development time and money you invested in it, prior to checking that the app gets accepted.

- Initial acceptance for a new app on the Apple App Store
  - At the time of press, less than 10 days
- Initial acceptance for a new app on the Google Play Store
  - At the time of press, less then 24 h

Updates for an already accepted app on both stores, providing the update is compliant, should take less than 48 h.

There is also store material that must be correct outside of the app development, including what you will need to do to get accepted on the different stores [27]. Store material will be discussed in Chap. 7: Budget/Project Management/Research/Marketing.

Digital Security

This topic includes the process of protecting digital information that is either crossing a network (data in motion) or is stored somewhere (data at rest). It is a huge topic requiring specialised expertise. In this section we aim to simply give you the fundamentals of understanding terminology and help you to grasp areas within the topic that must be considered to ensure that digital security within your app.

Data Protection[1]

There are lots of different ways of thinking about data protection. There are privacy issues, selling of data, personalized ads, losing data, getting hacked, etc. There are many questions to ask regarding your app and data protection.

- Are people getting more or less concerned about their personal data being public?
- Does the platform/device a person is using affect how they feel about data privacy?
- Is there a difference in how people in different countries see data collection?
- Are there laws regarding data collection in the market you are aiming for?
- Are there laws about selling people's data?
- If you have ads, what will advertisers want to know from you about your end users (personalized ads)?
- How often will you need to make updates and adjust code so that the data remains secure?

Here we are going to focus on teaching you how to make sure that people's data is secure and private and not inadvertently leaked. We will introduce you to the idea of thinking about people's data:

- How will it be stored?
- Where will it be stored?
- What regulations are there surrounding the storing of data?
- What is considered sensitive data?
- Is it different in different countries?

---

[1] The author of this book is not a technology security expert. This section is meant to give a basic overview.

Personal Data Protection

Increasingly, people are storing all of their personal data on mobile devices, which includes everything from health care cards, credit cards, pictures of driver's licenses, contact details, photos of their children (that contain metadata of where the photo was taken, and more. As an app developer, you must think about data security. Will the app you are developing store personal/private data? As a developer, you must do everything you can to make it secure.

Security and Vulnerability

Security and Vulnerability

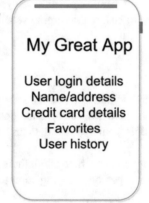

My Great App

User login details
Name/address
Credit card details
Favorites
User history

App security and vulnerability is an extremely complex and serious topic. Here, we will not aim to give you an in-depth lesson on these topics but to make you aware of the most important issues that you must consider when developing any app. We aim to make you aware of the basic terminology and the idea of securing data. Some would say that no app, website, server or any type of digital technology can be 100% secure at all times, but as a developer you must employ the latest techniques and do everything you can to ensure your end user's privacy and the safety of their data. You must also continually be aware of this topic and aim to keep your app up-to-date with the latest security measures.

We have broken this topic down into different topics that you must think about to make your app's data secure and private, both on the device and when going through the air or across a network. Software Development Environments will provide you with security APIs that you can use.

There are a few main things to consider:

- User Authentication, this is establishing a user's identity
- User Authorisation, this is selectively granting access to resources to an authenticated user
- Data security, this is both on data at rest and data in motion

- Integrity of the code being executed
  - https://developer.apple.com/documentation/security

Let's say you have developed a shopping app:

- What data gets stored on the user's device?
  - Internal data storage – data at rest
- What data is sent across a network?
  - Data in motion
- What data is stored off the user's device?
  - External data storage – data at rest
- How do you know it is the correct end user?
  - Authentication
- Can the user access any part of the game or, in a work situation, can they access all the files?
  - Authorization

Data Security

Sensitive data, such as a user's credentials and private information, should be protected by your app. This means making sure, when the app is developed, that security has been considered:

- Who should have access to sensitive data?
- Where is sensitive data stored?
- How will you authenticate a user's identity?
- How will you authorize access to various device/data resources

For a mobile app, these are the main topics that require security considerations:

- User credentials – authentication
- Authorization – rights and permissions
- Data at rest (internal/external storage)
- Data in motion (networks air/wired)
- Integrity check

You must make sure that all of these elements are secure for your end users.

Data at Rest

Whether you are storing data on a mobile device or storing it at a remote location, there are some things that you must consider. Do not share sensitive data, such as passwords or user credentials, with third parties. Think about sensitive data and

Fig. 5.13 Data in Motion

make sure that you are using the latest techniques to ensure that it is kept private. Do not allow sensitive data to be backed up, even by the mobile device's operating system. Both Apple and Android offer robust security measures that help you make sure sensitive data stays protected.

Conduct an internet search for Android and Apple documentation on security advice.

Data in Motion (Fig. 5.13)
Whenever data goes across a network, you should consider it to be vulnerable.

You should always send sensitive data (or even all data) using secure methods such as HTTPS.

Hardware Loss/Theft

Try to consider if a user were to lose or have their phone stolen. How would this affect your app? Is there a backup of data? Was this backup secure and did you remove all sensitive data before storing it? Is your app data safe now that it is in the hands of another person? Can the bad guy find out sensitive information simply by opening up your app? Did you use security measures for storing sensitive data on the mobile device?

Malware

Just like computers, mobile devices are susceptible to malware. There could be malware on your end user's device or even on a device that your app communicates with. Therefore you should presume that your app will come into contact with malware and develop standards that will protect sensitive data.

Enterprise Data

Personal mobile devices are increasingly being used for work/business usage. People do not give it a second thought to use a personal mobile device for work reasons, such as email or voice/video calls. In the past, places of business would have put a lot of time and effort into securing their business network by creating firewalls, etc. Now, however, an employee could easily be using a mobile device for business reasons on an unsecure open network. If it is your app that they are using, will this lead to a leak of sensitive data?

Authentication

Authentication

If you have any type of login to your app, you will require an authentication method. Authentication methods verify that the person logging in is indeed the correct end user. Deciding which authentication method will best suit your app will depend on how sensitive the data is that your app uses. This will determine how many layers of authentication you will need. Typically, apps that don't have much sensitive user information (for example, they don't store credit card details or social security numbers) will have a simple username and password, such as social media apps.

Even a simple password and username requires some thought though. Think about how often your app will be used by the end user? If it is frequently, they may remember their username. If it is infrequently, they may not remember it. Maybe using their email address as a username will be easier for the end user. Some would say this helps the end user remember their username, some would say that this might make the app less secure, as email addresses get scraped (stolen) from websites all the time.

Case Study The author has a staff user access to a university site. The policy is that staff must change their password every six months. You may not use a new password that is similar to any previous password. The author finds this so frustrating and difficult to remember (as they are not a regular user of the site) that they have told the university that they will write the password down on a post-it note and stick it on their computer. Which, of course, is a worst-case scenario as far as security goes and, of course, the author has not actually done this!

Do not push your end user so far that they become frustrated and bypass the security measures you are putting in place. Think about the end user and how tech savvy they may be. It may be better to have a simpler authentication system than have the end user writing down usernames and codes.

Currently there are three main ways to authenticate a user:

1. Information the user knows: such as passwords or PINs
2. Biometric data: such as fingerprint, voice, or face recognition
3. Information that is in the user's possession: such as through a digital certificate or tokens

2FA (two-factor authentication) means that two of these three methods are being used. There are other forms of authentication. Typically, apps that contain sensitive information such as bank apps will use 2FA.

There are some apps that must comply with strict authentication methods to be compliant with various government regulations and industry standards:

Financial apps will need to comply with the Payment Card Industry Data Security Standard (PCI DSS) [28].
Health care apps must comply with various standards according to different countries' compliance issues, such as HIPAA compliance [29].

There are methods of using a third party for authentication, such as using Google, Facebook, or the user's Apple ID to login. This can help users by reducing the burden of remembering yet another login/password, and it can also help you gain more users as they find it simple to login to your app. Search for the latest authentication and sign in documentation for companies such as, Apple, Google and Facebook.

Once a user has had their identity confirmed through authentication, as the app developer you will need to establish the rights and privileges for that user. You need to decide which permissions this user has. Authorization decides what the user can do, such as access a database, access a store, transfer money, etc. Companies such as Shopify provide free tutorials on using OAuth to grant authorization rights.

Of course, we have only scratched the surface here. Mobile app security is a whole field unto itself. If you want to find out more, you can begin with OWASP Open Web Security Project at https://owasp.org/ and look at their papers on Mobile Application Security.

Chapter Summary

This chapter introduced technology trends and hopefully you will now think about how technology trends could affect any app development that you may work on. This chapter also aimed to teach that there are other topics such as, compliance that you must have an understanding of, otherwise all your hard work could go to waste if your app was rejected. We also gave you a brief introduction into the complex world of data protection, security and data vulnerabilities.

Further Reading

Data security is a huge subject that requires a lot of research to be up-to-date. Search for the latest information by using these terms:

- Apple Authentication Services
- Apple Data Security Services
- Android Authentication Services
- Android Data Security Services
- Mobile App Data Security
- Mobile App User Authentication
- Mobile App Malware
- Data Validation Techniques

Take app store compliance seriously and research current compliance and review policy's for both Apple and Android.

Exercises

Exercise No. 16

Find an app that has had compliance issues with the App Store or Google Play Store. Write a short history of the app and original intention for the app.

- What is the name of the app?
- The app was developed in year X by X. By year X, it had X amount of downloads. The app was aimed at Y end users. It has evolved into Z. It has faced challenges from X, Y, Z. It resolved this issue by, it is still dealing with the issue by X...
- Are they currently on/off the App Store/Google Play Store?
- What does the future look like for the app?

Individual Reflection

To solidify your understanding in 500 words write out what you have learnt from this chapter. Here are some hints that you might use to write about.

- What does 'compliance' mean?
- What is digital security?
- What is authentications?

Knowledge Check

Fill in the blanks of the following sentence:
Use the words provided in the word bank.
.... is software that can be harmful to a computer system.
Data that is stored somewhere is termed .... Data that is moving across some type of network is termed.......................................
Apps must be .... to be accepted on to an app store.
Word Bank: Data in motion, Data at rest, Authentication, Compliance, Data security, Compliant, Acceptance, Digital security, Data protection, Malware, Authentication.

Answers

Below are suggested answers to the exercise given in this chapter. They are not complete and simply a suggestion to help you further think about your own solutions. You may well come up with a different or better solution. This is part of the app development process.

Exercise No. 16

Some apps that have faced compliance issues for a variety of reasons include:

- In Aug 2020 Fortnite the extremely popular gaming app was removed from the Apple's App Store for bypassing the App Stores in-app purchases. Fortnite bypassed Apple's system and implemented their own payment system.

Knowledge Check Answer

Malware is software that can be harmful to a computer system.
Data that is stored somewhere is termed **Data at rest**. Data that is moving across some type of network is termed **Data in motion**.
Apps must be **Compliant** to be accepted on to an app store.

Monetization

6

In this chapter we will look at a topic is less technical and more about the business side of app development. We will investigate how to make money from your app. The ability to make money from an app is called 'monetization'. Although monetization is very business centric, there is also some technical knowledge required to make sure that monetization work well. We will review the different ways there are to make money from apps. We begin by investigating what is monetization, how much money is spent on apps by end users, how money is being spent by companies or organizations on digital ads. Then we investigate eight different monetization strategies you can use to earn money from the app you plan to develop. Next we take a deeper look in how to incorporate ads into you apps and finally we look at some real life case studies to investigate what other apps used as monetization strategy and what the outcomes were.

Goal of This Chapter

In this chapter we aim to teach the fundamentals of how to earn money from different app designs and various approaches to applying techniques to earn money.

Vocabulary Introduced

- App economics
  - The range of economic activity that you can do to earn money from your app.
- Monetization
  - The process of earning money from an app.

T. Salter, *Technological and Business Fundamentals for Mobile App Development*, https://doi.org/10.1007/978-3-031-13855-3_6

- Monetization strategies
  - Different strategies that you can adopt within an app to earn revenue from the app.
- Demographics
  - Data that refers to your end user.
- Ad terminology
  - The various terms that Ad companies use to explain how to implement, earn money or how to receive payment.
- Ad agencies
  - Companies that provide your app with an ad.
- Ad revenue
  - The money that you receive in payout for including ads in your app.
- Ad Mediation company
  - A company that mediates on your behalf between multiple Ad Agencies.
- Freemium Model
  - A model whereby end users can download your app for free from an app store.

Levels of Understanding

Below in Fig. 6.1 we see a breakdown of knowledge required be able to understand the fundamentals of earning revenue from an app.

- We see the core knowledge required which covers topics such as different monetization strategies and how to determine the correct one for your end users.
- Expanded Non-Technical in this area requires a deeper understanding of how to conduct user research, how to apply advertisements to your app.

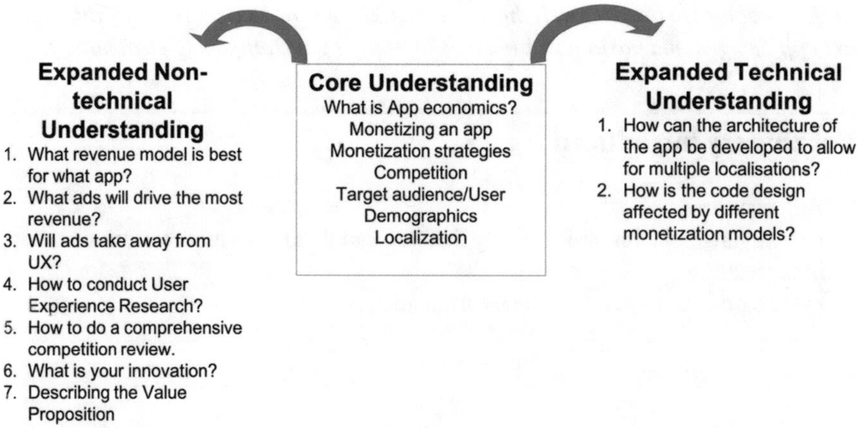

Expanded Non-technical Understanding
1. What revenue model is best for what app?
2. What ads will drive the most revenue?
3. Will ads take away from UX?
4. How to conduct User Experience Research?
5. How to do a comprehensive competition review.
6. What is your innovation?
7. Describing the Value Proposition

Core Understanding
What is App economics?
Monetizing an app
Monetization strategies
Competition
Target audience/User Demographics
Localization

Expanded Technical Understanding
1. How can the architecture of the app be developed to allow for multiple localisations?
2. How is the code design affected by different monetization models?

Fig. 6.1 Core, Non-Technical and Technical understanding for this Chapter

- Expanded Technical knowledge required including a deeper understanding of topics such as coding for localization to increase monetization potential.

Content

Monetization

App monetization is the process of making money from an app. There are various ways this can be achieved. Generally monetization strategies vary from one app to another. There is no 'one size fits all' solution that can be applied. All apps are different, and their monetization strategy must be thought out individually. This chapter will discuss the various forms of monetization. Your monetization strategy should be built into your app design from the beginning. You may not initially deploy your monetization strategy but you should know what it will be in the future so that you do not have to do a major overhaul of the UI/UX design of your app when you add the monetization strategy.

When thinking of monetisation we think a lot about business decisions but there is also technical work that goes into making this work well. All parties in the team, both technical and non-technical should know about the different monetization strategies available. This is however, a core knowledge needed by all and this is what this chapter will teach you.

There are some terms used in the domain of monetization of apps that everyone should be familiar with. Some of these terms span different ideas or concepts and they can be used in different contexts; therefore do not take these definitions as absolute. Here is a brief definition of the most common terms used in this chapter:

- **Monetization** – receiving revenue from an app by various means.
- **Acquired** – this is when a business or an app is acquired/purchased by another company.
- **Ads** – An advertisement that gets displayed in your app that you hopefully receive compensation for.
- **Screen Real Estate** – the size of a platforms screen.
- **Lite/Free app** – this is a cut down version of an app with less features than a version where the user must pay money.
- **Freemium** – this is a model where you provide the app for free and then charge for extras within the app.
- **In app purchases** – when you sell something physical or virtual in your app
- **Gated features** – parts of the app are gated or kept from certain users.
- **Premium** – Paid for apps.
- **Ad Network** – this is a company that will provide your app with ads.
- **Ad Mediation** – a company that sits between your app and multiple Ad Networks.
- **Upselling** – terminology used to identify a free app or a cheap app that you then charge more for at a later date.
- **Pay-to-install** – upfront payment for the user to be able to download the app from the App Store or Google Play Store.

- **Pay-to-subscribe** – recurring payment is required for the user to be able to continue using the app.
- **Recurring revenue** – revenue that comes in regularly.

Understanding App Revenue

There are many companies that offer statistics which assist in understanding revenues and business achievements of apps. App Annie [30] is a particularly well known company and they offer lots of insights into what apps are successful at earning revenue. You can use the App Annie website to look at revenue in various ways such as by regions, type of spending etc. Note: During publication of this book App Annie changed its name to Data.ai.

Mobile ad spending will top $290 billion in 2021 [31].

Tamoco gives us the 'Ultimate Guide to App Monetization' [32].

Ad Colony gives us many insights into the monetization, marketing and advising domains. They have various blogs about different topics that will give insights to the domain you are looking for [33].

The Business of Apps [34] gives us these statistics:

- Android and iOS app revenue reached $111 billion revenue in 2020, a 24 percent increase year-on-year. iOS was responsible for 65 percent of total app revenue in 2020
- Games accounted for 71 percent of total app revenue in 2020. iOS generated $47.6 billion revenue in 2020, while Google Play made $31.9 billion
- Outside of games, iOS was responsible for 76 percent of the $32.1 billion revenue created in 2020. Google Play generated $6.7 billion non-gaming revenue in 2020, to iOS' $24.7 billion
- Subscription revenues increased to $13 billion in 2020, iOS was responsible for 79 percent of this revenue

Paid and Grossing Apps

Two terms that are often used by companies that analyse app spending are 'Paid Apps' and 'Grossing Apps'.

- **Paid Apps** are usually the 'top paid for apps': This means the most downloaded apps that have a price tag greater than zero.
- **Grossing Apps** are usually the apps with the "highest total revenue.' This means the app could actually be free of charge but has something that is paid for within the app, be this a subscription or an in-app purchase. This type of app can be known as being a freemium app and top grossing apps may also include those that are earning revenue from advertising.

As we stated previously, there is a core level of knowledge that everyone on the team needs to know, whether they are technical or non-technical, and then a deeper knowledge within the various specializations required on both the non-technical and technical side.

Non-Technical Understanding

The non-technical or the business side of the app team should understand which monetization strategy will work best for the target market and the goals of the app. The non-technical decision makers should know about things, such as current trends in ad placement and ad types etc. They should make the decision on what ad company or mediation company is used. There is also a level of knowledge required to understand which monetization strategy will give the app the best return on investment (ROI).

Technical Understanding

The technical development team should know things, such as how to implement the chosen monetization strategy. What is the best way to implement this strategy to include flexibility for changes in the future? How to implement an ad library or how to implement mediation libraries. Implementing ad libraries can take time and skill. Programmers should know about things like current trends in things such as ad placement and ad type. Programmers should understand about screen real estate and how to best place the ad within the available screen real estate. If placement of the ad is done poorly and users repeatedly find that they accidentally click on the ad this can result in your app being refused ads by an ad company.

Revenue from Apps

Revenue from apps can come in different forms and have different terminology to break down and categorise this revenue. These are the most typical terms used:
- Paid apps
- Freemium apps
- Subscriptions
- Ad revenue
- In-app purchases
- Upselling

There is a way to breakdown and consider revenue from apps that separates passive income from end users (ads) and active income from end users (end user spending). If we use this form of breakdown it is possible to categorise revenue from apps in the following broad terms:
- End user spending - the money being spent by end users
- Advertising - the money earned through advertising revenue

End User Spending

End user spending covers anything that the end user pays for themselves. This includes paying for:

- In-app purchases of all kinds
- Subscriptions
- Paid for apps
- Upselling

When thinking about end user spending on apps it is important to understand how and what end users are spending their money on within the app world. This will give us an understanding of what actual end users pay for so we can apply this when deciding on a monetisation strategy. Global end user app spending is projected to climb to $270 billion by 2025 [35]. But one thing you can be sure of, is that the app world and how to make money from this world, is extremely fast paced and so you will have to keep up-to-date.

To further break down the end user spending on apps we can use terminology to categorise their spending. Often two terms are used, Premium apps and Freemium apps.

1. Premium apps have an up-front payment to download the app
2. Freemium apps can be downloaded free of charge. Their aim to generate income by others means, such as; in-app purchases, subscriptions or adverting.

Upselling involves getting the user to pay for something:

- Removal of ads
- The actual App
- Functionality
- A service

Advertising

Digital advertising is growing each year. It is now a serious form of advertising that all businesses, regardless of their focus, must consider, if they want to reach their audience. Now people routinely use digital media as a way to get their entertainment, news, to shop and much more. Those trying to reach an audience understand this.

When talking about digital media trends Deloitte, a global consultancy company said "The next wave of disruption may likely with Generation Z – who prefers to play video games, stream music, and engage on social media, rather than just watch TV or movies" [36].

Advertisers are increasingly using digital media as a way to advertise their products. The content or type of app you have developed may affect how much ad revenue you can earn. Apps with a very narrow user bases or very defined content such as alcohol or gambling may have difficulty filling ads. When considering how much ad revenue you may gross, think about the company wanting to advertise in your app. If you app content is very narrow it may only appeal to a very limited set of advertisers. For example, if you have developed a casino app you may find that large corporations that spend a lot on advertising may select 'do not advertise in money/ gambling' apps, therefore your app will not receive any ads from the corporation and as such, no ad revenue from them.

Below is a graph showing the Digital Ad spending worldwide (Fig. 6.2).

The above graph shows that a large sum of money is being spent on digital advertising. For you to be able to earn money from ads you must be able to implement them correctly and understand your end user.

Advertisers use targeting data to determine whether or not your app gets an ad. Targeting data includes things such as:

- Demographics (age, gender, location, economic status, etc. See the 4 Why's about knowing your end user)
- Application preferences
- Music passions
- Movie, TV and audio book genre interests
- Device (iPhone, Android)
- Network (Wi-Fi, 3G, 4G, 5G)

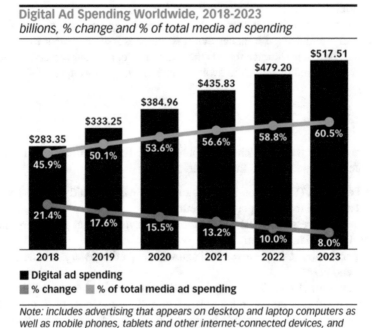

Fig. 6.2 Graph showing Digital Ad Spending. (Source: Graph published by https://www.mobil-eads.com/blog/mobile-advertising)

The more information you can glean about the end user who is viewing the ad within your app the more money you will be paid by the advertiser. This is common sense really; a company that is selling fast food may not want to advertise to the users of a dieting app. Therefore, the more knowledge you can give advertisers about your end users, the more advertisers can know how likely the end user will want the product they are advertising. If your end user is part of their target market, advertisers will pay a higher premium for advertising in your app.

How you incorporate ads in your app will either be a benefit or hindrance to your end user. Therefore, a lot of consideration should go into things such as

- Ad placement
- Type of ad that is displayed
- How often ads are displayed

Getting ads right is not as easy as you may think. You will need to give it a lot of thought. Research other apps in your genre that have successful ads. Don't over use ads; this can possibly interrupt the flow of a game or cause users to skip the ad, meaning you won't get paid.

There are even possibilities to first include ads by a geographical region to test ads on a smaller end user population for things such as user drop out. Take time to read and understand instructions from the Ad Network or Ad Mediation company that you use.

It seems that ads are particularly acceptable within the gaming market. Gamers do not seem to mind ads if it means that their game is free or cheaper to play. They do however, have a preference for ads that are more "contextualized and targeted to their preferences and they wish to avoid repetitive and irrelevant ads" [37].

Ad Terminology

There are various ways that an Ad agency/Ad Mediation company will calculate how much to pay you. This is the terminology they use.

- **Pay Per Click (PPC)** This is the amount you will get paid every time a user clicks on an Ad that is displayed in your app
- **Cost per Impression (CPI)** This is the amount you will get paid every time an Ad is displayed in your app
- **Cost per Action (CPA)-** How much you will get paid for every completed action by the end user.
- **Cost per View (CPV)-** This is the amount that you will get paid evert time a user watches a video or clicks on the video. Currently with Google Ads the end user must watch at least 30 seconds of the Ad or the whole Ad if it is shorter than 30 seconds long.
- **Click-Through Rate (CTR)-** The amount you will get paid each time the user clicks on an Ad
- **Cost per Mile (CPM)-** Payments for every thousand ad views.

- **Conversion Rate (CR)-** Percentage of users taking the desired action
- **Install Rate (IR)-** Percentage of users installing an app.
- **Ad Request** – First part of the ad process. Your app has requested to have an ad displayed within itself. However, an impression is not logged until after the ad has actually been displayed
- **Ad Impression** – An Ad is actually displayed to an end user
- **Fill rate** – The fill rate refers to the measure of an Ad being to delivered your app. There are many reasons an Ad might not be filled(delivered). There might not be an appropriate Ad available to fill. Perhaps your user is in a country that there are currently no ads for delivery (or filling).
- **Drop Off Rate** - The difference between Requests and Impressions
- **Click through rate (CTR)** – A measure of how often users click on your ads. If your ad receives one click per 100 views, you are said to have a CTR of 1% or .01. The higher your CTR - the higher your pay out per click
- **Cost per Click (CPC)** - Advertisers only pay when a user clicks on their ad. CPC payout is determined by the advertiser. Advertisers will pay more per click for sites with niche content
- **CPM** (cost-per-thousand) - Advertisers pay per thousand impressions to get their message exposed to a specific audience.
- **CPA** (cost-per-action) - Advertisers pay only for performance-based actions, like a user download.
- **eCPM** - Effective cost-per-thousand impressions. Expected earning per 1000 impressions. As there are many different advertisers etc. (eCPM) is the standard measure to compare relative advertising sources.

Two important factors to think of when choosing which Ad Network: eCPM & fill rate.

To work out what you will earn multiply eCPM by the fill rate. This calculation gives you the actual revenue earned per thousand ad requests.

Types of Ads

There are different types of ads which come in different formats, sizes and with different types of media. You should design a strategy that is likely to be the most successful for your end user/target market and the platform they are using. Ads can help you provide a better app either for free or at a lower cost but they can diminish the user experience and also take away from the screen real estate. You must find a blend of monetization that benefits both you and the end user. Here we look at the different types of ads that are available to you as a developer.

- Your primary responsibility is to design your user interface to accommodate space for advertisements. Therefore consider things such as:
  - Banner views use a portion of the screen to display the ad
  - Other types of ads can take the whole screen real estate and then return the whole screen real estate to the user

- You must include advertising without compromising user experience
- You don't want to drive your users away
- You can use tools provided by the Ad Network such as 'crash detection' to monitor if your ads are causing your end user any issues

Banner Ads

- These are the oldest type and most common type of ads. They are regularly used in advertising for mobile apps. Google calls these type of ad's 'Display Ads or Responsive Display Ads' [38]. Banner ads can be placed in different regions of the mobile device screen and can also be of varying sizes (see Fig. 6.3)

Interstitial Ads

- These are pop-ups that occur when the user tries to close the current page or they are trying to switch to a different page outside of the app (see Fig. 6.4)
- They cover the full screen, they often ask the user a question before they leave the app

Video Ads

- In-Stream – the video is equivalent to a commercial on TV. They play before or after the video/stream that the end user is watching. Often there is the option for the end user to skip the video after 5 secs (see Fig. 6.5)
- In-Display – this is a video that is displayed to the side in a Google search/ YouTube search etc. and the end user can click on it.

Fig. 6.3 Banner ads

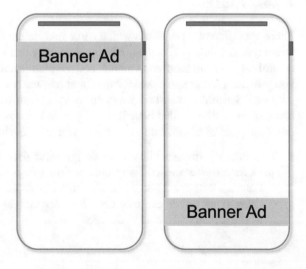

Fig. 6.4 Interstitial Ad

Fig. 6.5 Video Ad

Video ads can be used nicely if thought through properly. Find places within your app that are a natural break or transition such as, change in level of a game or natural breaks in work flow, and play the video ad there. Watching video ads can also be used as a reward. For example, if a player is out of lives they can get a new life by watching a video ad or, to continue watching content for free such as a TV show, they must first view a video ad.

Native Ads

- Whilst these Ads may appear similar to banner Ads they have a more 'native feel' about them. They are meant to appear as though they are part of the app
- They can be used in different ways such as sponsored content on an ecommerce site
- They can have a higher success rate than banner Ads as they are designed in a way that makes them feel like they are part of your app

Rich Media Ads

- These are Ads, typically of a banner type, that contain rich media such as a GIF or sounds or maybe some video
- They can appear more professional and appealing than banner ads

Below in Fig. 6.6: The ad changes, we see an ad in which the user receives an interactive experience. The user sees one image on their screen and then another image giving them a better experience.

Rewarded Ads

- Used in games, these ads offer the end user the opportunity to watch an Ad video in return for some reward, more coins, extra time etc.

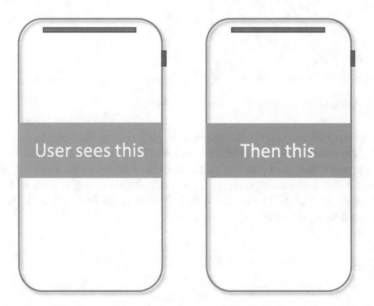

Fig. 6.6 The ad changes

- These Ads should be discoverable
- The user should easily be able to find the opportunity for the reward
- The user should feel that they get value from the reward [39]

Below in Fig. 6.7: Reward ads encourage the user to do something, we see how an ad can be placed to encourage the user to do something such as watch a video that we will in turn earn money for the app developer.

Implementing Ads

Including Ads can require more than a basic level of programming expertise to get them right but there will be lots of documentation to help achieve your goal of including a certain Ad Network into your app. You will need to add code to your app and the SDK of the Ad Network or Ad Mediation company that you are using. You will begin in test mode before going live so this will give you the ability to make sure the user will get the Ad experience that you want.

Here (currently in test mode) in Fig. 6.8: Showing placement of ad we see a banner Ad that is not perfectly filling the width of the screen but the placement of the ad is good as users are unlikely to accidently click on it.

Your Ad inclusion will require testing and tweaking to make sure that they give a good user experience.

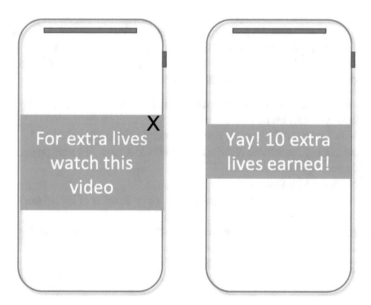

Fig. 6.7 Reward ads encourage the user to do something

Fig. 6.8 Showing
placement of ad

Ad Networks

There are many different Ad Networks for mobile advertising. An Ad network is a
company that will provide your app with ads. The Ad Network is the company that
businesses or people who would like to advertise go to in order to advertise to sell
their products. Probably the best well known is Ad Mob by Google.

- Ad Mob has just come out with a beta version of 'Real Time Ad Testing No Code
  Required' you can find a guide here [40]
- Smaato is another Ad Network that can send your app ads.
- You can simply search Ad Networks for mobile apps to various companies that
  provide your app with Ads.
- AdMob, owned by Google
- It enables you to serve ads in your app from any number of ad networks as well
  as your own house ads.
- Multiple networks enables you to determine which perform best for you and
  optimize accordingly.
- You get paid directly from the different ad networks

https://admob.google.com/home/

smaato

https://www.smaato.com/

Ad Mediation Companies

Ad mediation is the process of using a company that mediates on your behalf with various Ad Networks. The Ad mediation company will be connected with multiple Ad Networks and will use various methods to make a selection on how to serve your app with the best ad(s) for you (Fig. 6.9).

- Step one – your app sends a request for an Ad to the Ad Mediation Company.
- Step two – the Ad Mediation company sees what Ad Networks have the best ad for your app.
- Step three – the Ad Mediation company gets the Ad for you and sends it to your app (Fig. 6.10).
- The benefits of using an Ad Mediation company are that you will get a better fill rate for your Ad, you will likely increase your revenue and you will cut down on the amount of work it takes to manage various Ad Networks.
- You become less reliant on one network and can use multiple networks.
- It can cut down on a lot of coding as well.

Carry out research into current Ad Mediation companies and current techniques. Very well-known Ad Mediation companies include

- AdColony
- AppLovin
- InMobi
- IronSource
- Tapjoy

There are lots of others. Search to find the one that suits your needs.

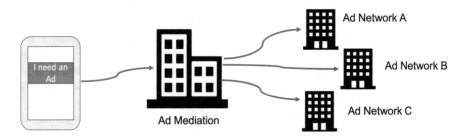

Fig. 6.9 App to Ad Mediation, Ad Mediation to Ad Networks

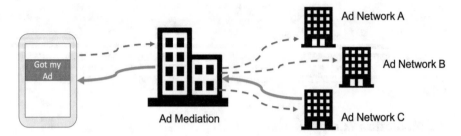

Fig. 6.10 Dashed blue line signifies a request for an ad. Green line signifies an ad request being fulfilled

Earnings

Your app will have to serve A LOT of ads for you to make any money. There are various ways to calculate how much you will earn.

Calculating Fill Rate

This is how you can calculate what your earnings would be from two different Ad Networks.

- Two ad networks, A and B.

  - **Network A:**

    - eCPM (see Ad Terminology) = $1.00
    - Fill rate (see Ad Terminology) = 80%
    - Revenue per thousand Ad requests = $1.00 × 80% = $0.80

  - **Network B:**

    - eCPM = $2.50
    - Fill rate = 25%
    - Revenue per thousand Ad requests = $2.50 × 25% = $0.62

Monetization Strategies

A monetization strategy will be based on many decisions, such as budget, why you are developing the app, time to launch etc. You may plan to develop an app on a smaller budget and then let users have it for free but include ads to generate revenue. Perhaps you plan to develop a very sophisticated app that you will charge for from the beginning and you have a large budget to cover development costs etc. Perhaps you have a long term strategy of developing a very sophisticated well designed app that will be free but will have some gated features.

When monetizing your app you will need to find a solution that is appealing to your end users. Some end users will want to not pay for the app and will expect having ads placed within the app. For some end users the annoyance of ads is great enough that they would rather pay to avoid the ads. For example, users may be prepared to pay a one-time fee or even a subscription to have the ads removed from their app. There are a lot of very sophisticated apps on the app stores that are either very cheap or use very well placed ads so that the end user does not have to pay anything for using the app. You will have to compete with these apps. If you want to charge for an app you will likely need to have an extremely sophisticated app that will require a lot of development and marketing money or have a very niche market. There must be a very compelling reason for a user to either pay for an app without having first sampled a free version or to pay for the app after having had a free trial (known as upselling).

Having a freemium app is a very popular solution to monetizing apps. Statisa tells us that "as of March 2021, almost 97% of apps in Google Play were free compared to 93% of apps in the Apple App Store" [41]. Business insider has said that "it is a race to the bottom" with regard to charging for apps [42].

End users now routinely expect very good apps at little or no cost.

Whilst this is not a definitive list, we have listed what are some of the most well-known monetization strategies that are currently used:

1. **None:** Altruistic, or an extension of a website/service
2. **Acquired:** Build a large audience & hope to get bought out
3. **Ads**: Apps that include Ads
4. **Freemium Model:** In-App Purchases: Sell something from the app
5. **Pay to Install:** Single up-front payment
6. **Pay to subscribe:** Pay a monthly or yearly subscription charge
7. **Free Trial:** Free trial for X amount of days
8. **Blended Models:** Deploy multiple strategies including various categories from above that are combined together

Strategy One: None

An App that is an extension of a brand/website/service etc. Perhaps you are being paid for developing the app. In this case you will need to know how to work out the cost of the project so that you know what to charge for the development of the app (see Chap. 7: Budget/Project Management/Research/Marketing). If you are developing an app as an altruistic endeavor, you must know how you will be able to afford to develop an app that is worthy of being used and make it useful to end users plus keep it updated etc. Again you will need to know how much it will cost you to develop it. In Chap. 7: Budget/Project Management/Research/Marketing we give advice on how to work out the cost of your project.

Strategy Two: Acquired

In this strategy you will need to prove that your app is used by enough people to make it worth being acquired by another company. You will need lots of end users either registered or signed up, or using your app in some form. There are lots of different reasons another company may want to acquire your app, they may see your app as a threat, or as a complimentary product to their app(s). For many different reasons lots of end users can be worth a great deal to another company.

In this scenario you will need to think about how you will get a large audience. How will end users discover your app (see Key Ingredient No. 4: Discoverability and Marketing in Chap. 7). This strategy can take a lot of money to achieve. In the following pages we look at some real life case studies that achieved this strategy. We look at when they launched, how much money they raised (investment) to achieve the outcome of being bought out. To achieve this will include having a company and raising funds from Venture Capitalists. In some cases you don't even need to have revenue or profit to be successful you just need a large user base. But if you have no revenue coming in you will need to be able to fund the project as well as any ongoing costs for support and updates until such time as the app is acquired see Chap. 7: Budget/Project Management/Research/Marketing.

- Instagram sold to Facebook for US $1 Billion (Wikipedia)
- Snapchat is currently valued in the range of 20 billion (Wikipedia)
- Twitter raised 1.2 billion with their IPO(Wikipedia)
- WhatsApp was purchased by Facebook for $19 Billion (Wikipedia)

Strategy Three: Ads

Including ads in your app can be a way to keep your app free for end users, whilst still enabling you to make money from your app. To make money from having ads in your app, will again require a lot of end users and preferably the end users using the app on a frequent basis. To make money from advertising you will need not only a lot of users, but a lot of end users that are prepared to sit through an ad. You do not get paid by advertisers for ads that users press the skip button on [43].

Some end users will even use ad blockers to stop the ad from running or popping up. As such you will not receive any revenue from these end users. Medium.com tells us *"For example, a YouTuber with a male audience primarily aged between 18 and 29 years old would likely have a higher percentage of viewers using AdBlock than a YouTuber with a female audience under 18 [44]"*.

Users will always find a way to block things they do not want, but this can require some technical knowledge. Ads are supplied to your app from a live internet connection, using cell data or Wi-Fi. This means users can tell their browser to not allow pop ups. It is even possible for advanced users to be able to block so called offline ads that downloaded from the internet and are built into your app.

Strategy Four: Freemium Model

The freemium model is the most used model for monetizing apps. The model consists of having a free app for the end user to download. This does not mean that the app will never make any money. In fact it can be the opposite as TechCrunch reported [45]. This app should be *missing functionality* or have *an annoyance.* Users pay to get the missing functionality or remove the annoyance. Think about what functionality that you can withhold, that the user, having tried the app will now pay for. This could be levels in a game, removing advertisements or paying to be able to go back in a dating app when you accidently swiped left, when you meant to swipe right.

In the freemium model you can use the following:

1. In app purchases - sell something from inside the app
2. Gated features - has some features that the user must pay to access
3. Upselling - has a free trial then charges for the app
4. Ads
5. Combination; any combination of the four above

End users seem to prefer the freemium model and they increasingly expect a high quality app with lots of features for free.

In-App Purchases

In-app purchases involve getting the user to pay for something from inside the app. This could be a one-time payment to unlock the full features of an app to regularly buying gold coins in a game. Apple states that there are three types of in-app purchases; *subscriptions, consumable purchases,* and *non-consumable purchases."* In this book we have separated subscriptions off into their own monetization model. Apple lists examples of consumable purchases as;

- Game currency, such as coins or gems
- Extra health points in a game
- A package of exports to a new file format

Apple lists examples of non-consumable purchases as

- Remove ads
- Full game unlock
- Upgrade to pro edition
- Bonus game levels

Apple's website has lots of information on in-app purchases.

It is possible to categorise in-app purchases in the following way:

- **Consumable:** Items that disappear after time/expire and need to be repurchased e.g. fire to keep you warm in a game or food for a virtual pet.
- **Functional:** Gives you some extra functionality e.g. in a game. Extra lives, or items within a game. Perhaps, virtual money to buy a house in a game?
- **Decorative/ Personalize:** Aesthetic/Let the user personalize the background, character, or other aspects of the game or app
- **Services/Subscriptions**: One off/Monthly/On-going. Access to a turn-by-turn map service. Subscriptions to digital magazines or newsletters

The freemium model can include upselling. See below in this section.

Gated Features

With holding functionality is sometimes called having gated features. This could be any type of functionality, such as pay to save your work, pay to print a page, pay to get full functionality.

Upselling

To upsell you provide a free or cheap version of the app as an enticement for a better version of the app. Your aim would be to get the end user to go from the free app to paying for in-app purchases or for paying to unlock features or to paying for a complete better version of the app.

A way to successfully implement the freemium model is to create artificial scarcity (see Glossary) for higher value items. You can even increase end user usage of your app by offering incentives for users who sign in frequently. Snapchat created the 'streak' which encourage users to communicate with each other every day. The 'streak' ends if you don't communicate with each other within 24 h.

Offer the user the paid for version to overcome annoyances/missing functionality. Users have been found resistant to even paying 0.99c especially in the beginning, so upselling can overcome this.

The business insider tells us "Generally speaking, having an IAP conversion rate (see Glossary) of 2-3 percent is considered pretty good [46]".

Strategy Five: Pay to Install

This strategy requires that the end user is either very familiar with the product (app) and they understand the benefits that they will receive from paying for the app or the app is very unique and they have no alternative.

Strategy Six: Pay to Subscribe (Pay Walls)

This strategy is very common with general media domains such as newspapers, magazines, music streaming, video streaming. Users seem comfortable paying subscriptions for media such as, video streaming services like Netflix or music services like Spotify. Subscriptions are usually something that must be paid regularly; monthly subscriptions are very common.

Strategy Seven: Free Trial

This strategy may suit apps that are aimed at media or work type apps. You let end users use the app for free for a period of time (X amount of days). After this the app becomes inoperable unless they pay to continue using it. This strategy is also very popular with subscription models. You will often get 30 days free trial and then you must pay to continue.

Strategy Eight: Blended Model

Many apps do use a blended approach by applying more than one of the above solutions.

Consider deploying multiple monetization strategies

- Free app
- Paid app
- Gated/Upselling
- In-App Purchases
- Advertising
- Sponsorship
- Buy Out

Of course, there are questions you must ask to work out which strategy will work best for an app. This is a list of basic questions you can ask to determine which strategy will best suit your goals for your app:

- **Strategy 1:** If you are being paid to develop the app you must work out the project cost so you make a profit. If you are developing an app as an altruistic endeavor, how will you fund the app if it is not generating revenue?
- **Strategy 2:** What makes you think you will acquire a large enough user base? How will you build a large user base? Marketing, ads, publicity? Why would a magazine write an article about you?
- **Strategy 3:** Where will the ads be placed? How will it affect your screen real estate? Will your end users accept having ads displayed?
- **Strategy 4:** What features will be gated?
- **Strategy 5:** What in-app purchases are you planning and why?
- **Strategy 6:** Why will people buy your app? What is the functionality that you will sell? Is your app so desirable that users would be willing to pay for it without trying it first? What about upselling instead?
- **Strategy 7:** What will you do and why?

Implementation

Manufacturers of devices want you to use their devices and therefore try to make it easy to achieve the monetization strategy you have chosen. The Integrated Development Environment (IDE) that you choose to use will likely offer software libraries or frameworks for you to easily implement monetization strategies. You implement In App Purchase in your iOS application using the Store Kit framework. This allows you to embed a store directly within your app.

Google provides a AdMob Guide which allows you to develop for several IDEs including iOS and Android. Both Apple and Android have strict advertising policies. You can find relevant information by searching Admob, Android and Apple advertising policies.

Chapter Summary

This chapter covered the fundamentals of how to earn money using different app designs. We introduced different approaches to applying techniques to earn money from apps while looking at different monetization strategies that can be applied and how advertising works with mobile devices.

Case Studies

Many apps begin life with one objective or goal which can change overtime. This can be seen with the evolution of certain apps. For instance, Facebook was originally started as picture catalogue of university students; it has morphed for many users into a news outlet, a public forum space, somewhere to find second-hand goods in your area. The company 'Facebook' has now morphed into a complete Meta Verse [47]. Angry Birds which was originally released as a fun game is now referred to as "Finnish action-based media franchise created by Rovio Entertainment" [48].

Angry Birds

Angry Birds was developed by Rovio Entertainment. Rovio was founded in Founded 2003 by Helsinki University of Technology students Niklas Hed, Jarno Väkeväinen and Kim Dikert [49], It was not until 2009 that Angry Birds was released [50]. What began as simple computer game has morphed into a complete entertainment and mechanising company. There are now movies, TV series, toys, multiple video games, clothing and even candy. In October 2017, Rovio shares were sold at NASDAQ Helsinki and the company was valued at $1 billion [51].

Instagram

Founded by Kevin Systrom and Mike Krieger in 2010, the company originally took in US$500,000 in venture capital seed funding in March 2010 [52]. The first Instagram post was in July 2010, four months after receiving the initial seed funding. Although where this post went to is unclear as the app was not released on iOS until October 2010 and was released on Android in April 2012 and a desktop version of Instagram was released in November 2012 [53]. Within one year of the Oct

2010 launch of the iOS version it had over one million users. January 2011 added #tags to help users discover both photographs and each other. April 2012 saw the launch of the Android version (downloaded > one million times in less than one day). April 2012 Instagram raised $50,000,000 in venture capital. April 2012, Facebook offer US$1Billion in cash and shares for Instagram. Deal closes September 6, 2012 Raised $57,500,000 from VCs to get there. $0 revenue prior to Facebook buyout [53, 54].

Twitter

Twitter was first publicly available July 15, 2006. It was developed by a podcasting company and an undergrad from New York University. 2007 at South x Southwest Interactive usage increased from 20,000 tweets per day to 60,000. Twitter placed two 60-inch plasma screens in the conference hallways, exclusively streaming Twitter messages. 2016: 500 million tweets per day. 60% of tweets sent from mobile devices. Raised over US$57 million from venture capitalist, although exact numbers are not publicly disclosed [55]. Reportedly when Twitter did its Initial Public Offering (IPO) it was more than Google's [56].

Snap Chat

Whilst all studying at Stanford university, Reggie Brown, Evan Spiegel and Bobby Murphy created Picaboo for iOS in July 2011. TechCrunch tells us that the idea came from being able to post pictures that would disappear [57]. Within months of Picaboo being formed Brown was ousted from the company [58]. The company was rebranded as Snapchat and was relaunched on iOS in Sep 2011 and on Android Oct 2012. After negotiating though lawyers Brown settled with Spiegel and Murphy for $157.5 million in Sep 2014.

The general idea behind Snapchat is still to send friends photos or videos that exist for a set length of time. *"Snapchat isn't about capturing the traditional Kodak moment. It's about communicating with the full range of human emotion — not just what appears to be pretty or perfect"* [59]. Snapchat was presented as a solution to the stresses caused by the longevity of personal information on social media, evidenced by *"emergency detagging of Facebook photos before job interviews and photos* [47] *hopping blemishes out of candid shots before they hit the internet"* [59].

Snapchat raised slightly less than 3 billion in funding in the first five years since it was initially founded; exact figures are hard to discover [60]. In 2014 Snapchat acknowledged the need for a revenue stream and announced it would begin including advertising in its platform [61]. In 2017 it went public with an Initial Public Offering (IPO) on the New York Stock Exchange on Thursday, March 2, selling 200 million shares priced at $17 per share, for a total of $3.4 billion. The share price rose to a little over $24 by the end of the day, corresponding to a market cap of $33 billion [59, 62, 63].

Wordle

After reading the above case studies it can seem like a daunting task to be able to develop an app that can become a great success. However, Wordle is the perfect example of how it is still possible to begin very small or alone and still make it big.

Wordle was created by Josh Wardle in October 2021. The game became popular in December 2021 after Wardle added the functionality for players to be able to post their daily results. In January 2022 the game was purchased by The New York Times for an undisclosed seven-figure sum [64].

Exercises

Exercise No. 17

From the case studies above write out the following (you do not need to be exact):

- How long does it take for apps to gain revenue?
- Do all apps have to raise money from Venture Capitalists?
- Which app raised the most money?
- What was the longest and shortest duration for the original app to be acquired?

Individual Reflection

To solidify your understanding in 500 words write out what you have learnt from this chapter. Here are some hints that you might use to write about.

- What are the different monetization strategies that can be applied to apps?
- How do you calculate what you will earn from including advertising in your app?
- What is a freemium app and how could you make money from it?

Knowledge Check

Fill in the blanks of the following sentence:

Use the words provided in the word bank.

The process of .... helps you gain revenue from your app.

Having a .... will help you develop your app in such a way to have the maximum potential to earn revenue. An .... works with various Ad agencies to provide ads to your app. The process of withholding some functionality within an app is sometimes known as having ....

Word Bank:

App economics, Monetization, Monetization strategy, Competition, Ad agencies, Gated features, Ad revenue, Ad Mediation company, Freemium Model.

Answers

Knowledge Check Answer

The process of **Monetization** helps you gain revenue from your app.

Having a **Monetization strategy** will help you develop your app in such a way to have the maximum potential to earn revenue. An **Ad Mediation company** works with various Ad agencies to provide ads to your app. The process of withholding some functionality within an app is sometimes known as having **Gated features**.

Budget/Project Management/Research/Marketing

7

The creation of high quality software, delivered on time and on budget, requires careful planning and execution. You will need to manage your project end to end to make sure your app is developed, uploaded to the app stores, accepted and that it is available to end users. You will then need to make sure that end users know about your app, download it and use it. All of this will require project management skills.

Project management skills mean having the ability to understand the whole of your project. You must go through a series of steps and perhaps use developed methodologies to help you break up the project into manageable, logical sections.

You can get a lot of advice and help from official associations that specialize in project management. It will benefit you if you become familiar with the terminology used within project management. The Project Management Institute has certifications in well-known project management methodologies. Visit

- https://www.pmi.org/certifications/agile-acp

Goal of This Chapter

Here we aim to give you the key components required to be able to successfully manage your project. There is a lot of work that surrounds a successful app outside of the actual app development. There are many factors and areas that you will need knowledge of to successfully develop, produce, upload, and finally have target end users using your app.

Vocabulary Introduced

- Scheduling
  - The process of taking a series of steps in a defined way
- Methodologies

© The Author(s), under exclusive license to Springer Nature Switzerland AG 2022
T. Salter, *Technological and Business Fundamentals for Mobile App Development*, https://doi.org/10.1007/978-3-031-13855-3_7

- • Methodologies are systems that have been tried and tested.
- • Agile, Scrum and Project Life Cycle
  - • These are very well known project management tools
- • Budget
  - • Every project needs a budget for different parts of the project.
- • Testing and evaluation
  - • How to test your app and evaluate if it meets the original criteria
- • Surveys & Questionnaires
  - • Tools for survey your end users
- • Analysis
  - • Analysing the data gleaned from your surveys
- • Marketing
  - • The process of promoting your app.
- • Competition
  - • The other apps that are similar to yours or that in some way compete with you in your chosen app domain.
- • ASO (App Store Optimization)
  - • The process of using tools to increase the visibility of your app on any app store.
- • In-app analytics
  - • Data that can be obtained from your app such as GPS data or user behaviour.
- • Store Material
  - • The material that you must produce for any app store to get your app accepted on to the store.

Levels of Understanding

Below in Fig. 7.1: Core, Technical, Non-Technical understanding for Chp. VII we see a breakdown of the knowledge required for this subject into categories. This knowledge will help you effectively manage an app development project. This information will help you consider budgets for different areas of the app development project.

- • We see the core knowledge required which covers topics such as Marketing, ASO, Research and Analysis and Project Management.
- • Expanded Non-Technical in this area requires a deeper understanding of Time frames, how to conduct end user research, when to release your app etc.
- • Expanded Technical knowledge required including a deeper understanding of topics such as implementing app analytics SDKs and how to maintain an app.

Expanded Non-technical Understanding	Core Understanding	Expanded Technical Understanding
1. What marketing tools will you use to promote the app (CRM's)	Marketing & tools	1. What marketing tools can you deploy to help the marketing team (php scripts for mass email marketing etc)?
2. User acquisition (UA)	ASO	
3. Will ads take away from UX?	App store material	2. Knowing how to implement In-App Analytics SDKs
4. How to conduct the most beneficial user research?	In-app Analytics	3. Implementing Social Share from within the app
5. Time Frame - How to break it down.	Research & Analysis	4. How much maintenance will be needed to keep the app functioning and relevant?
6. Planning time of each component to the whole	App Maintenance	
7. When to release	Branding	5. Website hosting, domain provider/Servers
8. When to expect revenue	ASO	
	In-app analytics	
	How app store categories affect app downloads	
	Budget/Project Management	

Fig. 7.1 Core, Technical, Non-Technical understanding for this Chapter

Content

The development of any app requires the following of a schedule, methodology, outline or steps to be taken. We gave a series of steps to follow in Chap. 1: Overview of Steps and Necessary Skills. These steps are aimed more at the project as a whole and less about the development of the app. The steps given here include project management and thinking about budgets etc.

Not following a series of steps will result in an Inferior app. We cannot say for sure the steps you will require to produce your app or what will be best order in which to apply the steps. We give the following examples of project management as a guide.

Scheduling

Every project must be scheduled, whether this will include timelines on how long you will spend on coding, marketing, research and analysis. You should have a schedule and regularly check if you are meeting your scheduling goals.

Methodologies

Methodologies are systems that have been tried and tested. There are different methodologies for different areas of study. Here we list two of the best known methodologies for project management of software systems (Agile and Scrum Methodologies) and a standard methodology used for general project management (Project Life Cycle).

Agile Methodology

Agile project management is a very commonly used methodology within the domain of project management. In software development it is probably the most well-known methodology. Agile development involves using a series of methods to discover requirements and find solutions for improvement. This is achieved by a collaborative effort of a team. Agile methodology is a system of continuous iteration of testing and development throughout the whole of the project life cycle or software development process.

The Agile Methodology is based on twelve principles [65].

1. Customer satisfaction
2. Welcome changing requirements
3. Deliver working software frequently
4. Close, daily cooperation between business people and developers
5. Projects are built around motivated individuals, who should be trusted
6. Face-to-face conversation is the best form of communication
7. Working software is the primary measure of progress
8. Sustainable development, able to maintain a constant pace
9. Continuous attention to technical excellence and good design
10. Simplicity
11. Best architectures, requirements, and designs emerge from self-organizing teams
12. Regularly, the team reflects on how to become more effective, and adjusts accordingly

Scrum

Scrum project management is another very commonly used term. Scrum.org [66] tell us *"Scrum is a framework within which people can address complex adaptive problems, while productively and creatively delivering products of the highest possible value."*

Scrum methodology involves working in short manageable cycles that are called sprints. Sprints are supported by daily team meetings where tasks are reviewed and issues are discussed.

Project Management Software

You can also use various types of software designed to help you manage your project. These can be as simple as using PowerPoint to make Gantt Charts to software specifically designed for technology project management such as, Slack. This is a communication tool to help manage projects https://slack.com/. Smartsheet is a project management tool that increases typical spreadsheet functionality to include functionality for project management https://www.smartsheet.com/ .

Project Life Cycle Methodology

Typically when discussing the Project Life Cycle people will talk of four phases:

1. Initiate
2. Define
3. Execute
4. Closing

Each of the phases of the project life cycle itself can have steps and it is possible to reiterate over these phases. These phases are intuitive, you must initiate the project, think of the idea, then plan how will you handle the project as a whole, then you begin to execute the project, bringing all your planning and ideas together, finally you complete or close the project. In reality with app development the project will never be finalised or closed. You will continue to have work on the project staying up to date with new technologies, trends in UI/UX etc (Figs. 7.2 and 7.3).

Project Life Cycle Methodology

Typically when discussing the Project Life Cycle people will talk of four phases:

1. Initiate
2. Define
3. Execute
4. Closing

Fig. 7.2 Project Life Cycle as a whole gives a visualization of how break up the project from an entirety into the four phases

Fig. 7.3 Project Life Cycle as a whole

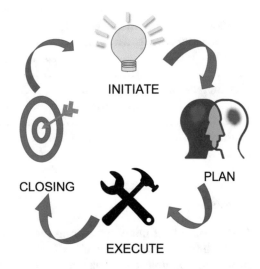

Project Life Cycle Phase One: Initiate

You will have the idea for an app or will be given an idea to develop for someone else. Perhaps you work for a company and you are told that the company would like to move to having a mobile app for their business. Begin with working out was is the idea, what is the app meant to do, what are the goals for the app.

Project Life Cycle Phase Two: Plan

Begin by thinking of the project as a whole. For example, how complicated is the app that you are developing? Make sure to read Chap. 1: Overview of Steps and Necessary Skills. Breakdown the projects as a whole into tasks that are manageable and think about how long will each tasks take.

Examples of tasks might be:

- Outline app functionality make sure that it has the Key Ingredients
- Outline the Four Ws
- Calculate Budget
- Technology requirements
- Skills
- Graphics
- Monetisation Strategy
- Research competition
- Marketing

Follow the below steps to help you create an amazing app.

Steps

App Title..

Functionality ....

The Four Ws..

....

Key Ingredients..

....

....

Features..

....

Budget

Budget will affect many things and the decisions you will have to make. How much budget you have may affect things like when you need to gain revenue from your app and so this may affect your monetization strategy.

What hardware do you need for development?
What software do you need for development?
What servers are there and what are their costs?
Website hosting, domain provider?

Overall Budget...
Broken Down:
Software Development ....
Hardware ....
Graphics..
User Testing...
Marketing...

Equipment/Technology Resources Budgeting

- Technical costs
- Hardware
- Server/Data costs
- Software costs/Github, website etc.
- Non-Technical costs
- Marketing/Graphics/Design Costs
- App Store(s)/Business
- Time Frame
- Legal Issues

Think about the hardware and software you will need to complete your project. Include things such as an Apple developer license in North America costs $99 (yearly). You will need not only an Apple laptop but also an Apple iOS device e.g. iPhone to produce the binary file for the app store.

Equipment List for Technology Requirements

Hardware	....	Cost..............
Hardware	....	Cost..............
Hardware	....	Cost..............
Hardware	....	Cost..............
Software	....	Cost..............
Software	....	Cost..............
Software	....	Cost..............
Software	....	Cost..............
Software	....	Cost..............

Monetization Plan

What will be your monetisation plan? How quickly do you need to get revenue in? Read Chap. 6: *Monetization* to help you decide on your monetization strategy will be.

Monetization Strategy Number ....
Notes...
....
....

Project Life Cycle Phase Three: Execute

Thinking back to Chap. 1: Overview of Steps and Necessary Skills, what are the skills you have to execute this plan? What people do you need to bring on-board to execute the plan. To execute this plan you will need to go over all the other chapters in this book. Once you are happy with your idea/app you will need to test it on end users. These are the extra steps necessary to execute an app development plan.

Research

Competition

You will always have competition. Make an analysis of your competition. What other apps are there in your field? What makes yours different? Ask yourself these questions:

- What is unique about your app?
- What are your competitors doing?
- What is great/what isn't great in your competitors app?

Case studies of logos and names for popular apps.
   How the logo and name affect apps.

Case Study

When beginning the idea for a communications app for Citizen Alert Inc., we first formulated the functionality/features of the app and decided who was our main target market and then we conducted market research on our competition.
   We looked at North American companies as our main target market was small towns in North America. We investigated as series of key words to find companies that were already functioning within our chosen market. After extensive searching that we had 16 genuine competitors. We then compared our key features (see Key Ingredient No. 8: Features) with these 16 competitors key features of their app systems.
   We made a spreadsheet with headings (see Fig. 7.4: Spreadsheet of competition for the Citizen Alert communication system.) that were relevant to the aims, goals and features of our planned communication app/system.

Fig. 7.4 Spreadsheet of competition for the Citizen Alert communication system

We used the following headings for our spreadsheet:

- Competitor
- Competitor URL
- Branded
- Notifications
- Alerts
- Customizable for Town
- Customizable for End User
- Their target market
- Focus of their system
- Extra functionality/Features
- Two-way communication
- Geo-fencing
- Multilingual
- Registration Required
- Integrations (other APIs)
- Estimate of current number of users
- Pricing model

Testing and Evaluation

It is very important to make sure you fully know your end user (see Chap. 2: Key Ingredients for a Great App). When you know who your end user is you can then you can test your initial app design in mockup form (see Chap. 3: *Concept Design*) on your target market. This will be an iterative process, make sure you learn from this process and use the information to improve your app.

You will need to take a series of steps to achieve your goal of learning from your end user.

- Why are you conducting the research?
- How will you conduct your research?
  - This may be different for different stages of your app. For example
  - Step One Research: You may begin by setting up an online survey with screenshots of a graphical mockup of your app.
  - Step Two Research: After some initial research and further development you may need to find a way to provide your potential end users with a working prototype of your app.
- What do you hope to learn from the research?

- How will you analyse the findings from the research?
- How much research will you conduct?
  - Do you have a timeline?
- How much budget do you have for research/user testing?
- How will you implement and test any changes needed to your app?

Thinking about these questions can help you formulate a plan to help you test your app on your end user and how to learn from this process.

There are various ways to test your app designs on your end user. Hubspot [67] provides free templates for conducting questionnaires. There are various kinds of questionnaires and questions that you can use to research how your end user(s) feel about your app. There are various types of questions each have their own uses, advantages and even some disadvantages that you can use to create a questionnaire.

Surveys and Questionnaires

A questionnaire is just one type of tool that you can use to survey your end users. The aim of a questionnaire is for you to get feedback from end users. They help you see your app from another's point of view.

A survey is the process of gathering information and analysing this information. This could involve taking the information gleaned from questionnaires, plus analysing and interpreting this data to give the survey results.

There are many tools that are either free or very cheap that you can use to survey your potential end users. Companies such as SurveyMonkey [68] provide very easy to use tools to help you create surveys and questionnaire.

Develop your questionnaire with questions that will give you insights into whether your app fulfils its goals for the end user.

- What types of questions will you use?
  - Open-ended
  - Multichoice
  - Rating scale
- How will you ask the questions? In person or set up an online questionnaire?

Questions

When you are thinking of the questions you want to ask your end user. Think about how many you want to ask, what is really important, how long will it take the end user to answer? Make a list of questions and then see if this covers everything you need or is to comprehensive? Some participants may be happy to spend time giving you feedback others may want to do it quickly.

Try to keep any questions that you ask unbiased. Do not lead the end user to your own conclusions. Remember you are trying to learn from the end user.

The names of the most common types of questions are:

- Open questions
- Closed questions

- Multiple choice questions
- Dichotomous questions
- Rating questions
- Ranking questions

Open Ended Questions

These types of questions require the participant to answer the question with their own words. Some people prefer being able to give their opinion rather just ticking boxes. You can gain a lot of insight and also often be surprised by the answers those you are surveying will give. It can sometimes help you in ways you would have never thought of. The types of words to include in open ended questions include:

- How
- What
- Explain
- Why
- Describe

Examples of open ended questions are:

- Could you tell us **how** we could improve our app?
- **Why** would you download a recipe app?
- **What** are the main features you would look for from a recipe app?

The process of analysing the results from open ended questions is called qualitive research and can be a lot more time consuming than analysing the results from other types of questions.

Closed Questions

Examples of close ended questions are:

- Have you ever used a recipe app? YES/NO if yes go to multiple choice Q1
- If No is it something that you might consider YES/NO if yes go to multiple choice Q2

Multiple Choice Questions

Examples of close ended questions are:

- Q1 When did you use a recipe app
  - Only for special occasions
  - I use a recipe app at least once a month
  - I use a recipe app Weekly
  - Only for very complex recipes

- Q2 Pick the feature that you would most want in a recipe app
  - Recipes type food groups
  - Recipes for cultural foods
  - Recipes for weight management
  - Recipes for different budgets
  - Recipes based on length of time

Analysis

Once you have conducted some research and participants have answered your questions you will need to analyse the responses. For non-open ended questions you can use a variety of different tools including charts and graphs. For open ended questions you use text analysis to find common responses but you may choose just to simply read open ended questions and note down commonalities or important issues that you find.

Report

Make a report of your findings from your market research. Report what you have learnt from the end user surveys. Have you answered any questions that you had about functionality, features, look of your app? Was there anything that you had not initially thought about that should now be added as a feature of your app? Perhaps you discovered that a feature should be removed due to over complicating your app. Report all your findings.

Project Life Cycle Phase Four: Closing

This could be the moment that you upload your app to the app stores. The reality of the fast paced ever changing app/technology world means that the project life cycle of your app may be unlikely to actually be closed, the initial phases of the development may close and then maintenance may begin.

We may suggest that you employ an iteration strategy and go over the project life cycle again after you feel that you reached Phase Four.

Submission/Store Material

You will have to produce the material required by the app stores. Your material for your app will be a crucial first impression to your target market. This will include various sized icons, written information and screenshots of your app. Both Apple and Google Play will help you with how to create the marketing material you will need to their respective stores. Apple has lots of documentation and guides on how to effectively produce App Store Material to help your app be seen in the best light possible.

The development of your app store material will help with the marketing of your app. Your app store material should be a true an accurate reflection of your app's functionality and features. A reason for this is that user reviews can greatly affect an app's popularity. It is a priority for end users to get an app that they expect from what they see in the app store material.

Requirements for app stores are as follows:

- Screenshots
- App Icon
- Feature graphics
- Writing a description of an app

Keywords and Key Phrases

- Localizing material
- What category do you want your app placed in?

Branding

You will get a lot of information about how your app should be branded from the exercises you carry out in Chap. 2: Key Ingredients for a Great App and also from Chap. 3: *Concept Design*. Just like the concept design of your app, the branding and logo design should be relevant to your target market. You will need to create a logo and name that reflect either what to expect from your app, for example, Simple To Do List or a logo and name that speak to your target market, for example, Uber.

Marketing

There is a lot to marketing. A simple Google search for the term 'Marketing Basic' will show you the vast complexity of this subject. This book hopes to teach you that you must take marketing seriously. Your app is very unlikely to be a run-away success without marketing.

There are many companies and tools that can help you market your app. How you market your app will depend on who your end user(s) are and what your target market is.

Marketing as a whole has many sub domains:

- Social Media Marketing
- Email Marketing
- Product Launches
- Brand management

The list of sub domains goes on and is really a factor of budget and resources.

Companies like Hubspot [67] will provide you will marketing and customer relation tools to help you keep track on how you market your app.

Make a basic marketing plan to include things such as:

- How will you market your app?
- What methods will you use?
- What tools are available to market your apps?
- Can you use in-app analytics?
- Can you use your own app to help market itself by allowing users to share about it on social media?
- Market Analysis.
- What marketing tools will you use to promote the app (CRM's), see how long people use the app for, download rates.
- What marketing tools can you deploy to help the marketing team (php email scripts)?
- What tracking technologies can you build into the app to help the marketing team?
- How can you code social share buttons
- How much maintenance will be needed to keep the app functioning and relevant?

What marketing tools can you deploy to help the marketing team (php scripts for mass email marketing)?

There are other ways to promote your app such as using influencers. How you can promote your app will depend a lot on your budget.

You will likely also need a website that will also need to optimized so as to increase Search Engine Optimization (SEO) and visibility. You will need to check that your domain/website hosting allows for things like 'XML site map' upload and other SEO tools.

ASO (App Store Optimization)

ASO is the same principle as SEO (Search Engine Optimization), the difference is that you are trying to optimize your app visibility in an app store rather a website's visibility in a search engine. You will need to think about ASO. By considering ASO you hope to increase your app's visibility in an app store, making sure that your app is seen when people search or browse an app store. Hopefully this in turn leads to an increase in downloads of your app. To achieve a high or successful ASO will involve using the correct keywords or key phrases in your app store material. When your app reaches a high enough level of downloads it will feature more strongly in an app store's charts. This in turn will increase your ASO. In the begin it can be hard to feature anywhere near the top in an app stores. This is because you need lots of downloads to feature at the top of app store listings.

Choosing the right category for your app will also affect how likely it is to appear in app store search results. Certain categories (such as Games) require a huge amount of daily downloads for an app to be listed in search results.

In-App Analytics

In-app analytics is the process of gaining data on the usage of your app. As with everything within the mobile development world things change quickly and often. From iOS 14.5 onwards Apple Inc. implemented Apps Tracking Transparency.

Do a search for the current status of 'Apps Tracking Transparency'.

Google Analytics provides a free SDK for both Android and iOS mobile apps to enable you to carry out in-app tracking. Go to the Google Developers website to find the SDK and information on how to implement it.

SDKs like this can be implemented within your app and are only useful once a user has downloaded, installed and launched your app.

In-app analytics can give you information about what a user does within your app. You can gain insights into metrics such as amount of users, device information, user behavior, user demographics, user retention, session duration and geo location data.

Track events:

- It is possible to track how users interact with your app. This will help understand things like how users navigate through your app which can give you insight as whether your app is designed well or users are getting lost inside your app.
- By incorporating an analytics SDK it is possible to assign important 'events' or 'actions' within your app and the analytics software will track when a user carries out these events.

Spending within the app
- It is possible to track user spending with apps. You can monitor ecommerce activity and then of course combine this with other factors that you have chosen to track within your app.

Goals
- It is possible to define 'goals' within analytic software. You can then track whether your goals are being achieved. Examples of 'goals' might be, to reach a certain level in a game, or click a purchase button for a promoted item within social media app. You can then view 'Goal' reporting on your analytics dashboard.

Custom metrics
- It is possible to define custom metrics within your analytics code to collect data that is custom to your needs. What you can collect is dependent a lot on how your app is coded. For example if you required that your user register an account with and give age and gender information. Then this information can be turned into a custom metric when combined with tracking about what level a player reached in a game. You may be able to ascertain how the game is performing for different age groups or genders.

Chapter Summary

Here we looked at some of the key components required to be able to successfully manage a project. We introduced you to the work that surrounds managing the project of a successful app development. We hope that you now have an appreciation for the factors and areas that you will need knowledge of to successfully develop, produce, upload, and finally have target end users using your app.

Case Study

Wordle

Wordle is a web-based word game developed by Josh Wardle [69]. At the time of publication this game is extremely popular. It is hard to not come across the game, from TV or radio presenters discussing it, to seeing your friends and family posting their successes at the game on social media or electronic forms of communication.

The is a great example of how thinking about marketing and features of an app can make an app successful. Wikipedia tells us that "Wardle initially created the game for himself and his partner to play, eventually making it public in October 2021. The game gained a large amount of popularity in December 2021 after Wardle added the ability for players to copy their daily results as emoji squares, which were widely shared on Twitter" [69].

Exercises

Exercise No. 18

Conduct some market research on an app of your choice. Look at the competition for the app. Does it have a lot of competition?

Create a questionnaire to ask potential end users questions about what they think of a graphical mockup that you invent. Use user flow diagrams to help you imagine what questions you might ask an end user about your mockup.

Analyse what the end users say. Did they get the same feeling from the app that you aimed at. Did they find it easy to use? Did they give you any insight into how you could improve your app? Would they use your app?

Individual Reflection

To solidify your understanding in 500 words write out what you have learnt from this chapter. Here are some hints that you might use to write about.

- Why should you use project management skills during your app development process?

- What is ASO?
- Why is marketing important?

Knowledge Check

Fill in the blanks of the following sentence:

Use the words provided in the word bank.

A way to test whether your app is suitable for your target market is by conducting target user ……………… To conduct a survey you can use tools such as a …………………….. Once you have gathered the information from the survey you will need to conduct ………………. Every app will have some …………….. you should research them to see how you can differentiate yourself from them. Performing ………………. helps your app to be visualized on different app stores.

…………….. help you understand how your users are using your app and if it fulfils the goals you set out.

Word Bank:

Competition, Surveys, Questionnaires, Budget, Marketing, Survey Analysis, Store Material, App Store Optimisation (ASO), Competition, Testing and evaluation.

Answers

Knowledge Check Answer

A way to test whether your app is suitable for your target market is by conducting target user **Surveys**. To conduct a survey you can use tools such as a **Questionnaires**. Once you have gathered the information from the survey you will need to conduct **Survey Analysis**. Every app will have some **Competition** you should research them to see how you can differentiate yourself from them. Performing **App Store Optimisation (ASO)** helps your app to be visualized on different app stores.

Testing and evaluation help you understand how your users are using your app and if it fulfils the goals you set out.

Conclusion

We are excited for the world to have your new app. We hope that this book helped you in many ways. Read each of the chapters even if you do not feel it is relevant. All of the information contained in this book is relevant to everyone involved in app development.

Good Luck!

T. Salter, *Technological and Business Fundamentals for Mobile App Development*, https://doi.org/10.1007/978-3-031-13855-3

Below is a list you to help you think about your project as a whole.

Project Task List

Task ....

Length of Time.............. Complete by ....

Budget ....…..

Skills requirements...

....

Person in charge ....

Notes..

....

....

Task ....

Length of Time.............. Complete by ....

Budget ....…..

Skills requirements...

....

Person in charge ....

Notes..

....

....

Glossary

In this book we will use the following terminology. As with all software development the lines between definitions can be blurred at times

- **Apps** – any software application, but for this book meaning a software application downloaded by a user to a mobile device.
- **Artificial Scarcity** – a term used to suggest to users of an app that an item they want may not always be available and may be in high demand.
- **BaaS** – Backend-as-a-Service
- **Back End Developer** – a tech person that works on the back end of websites or apps. They work with things such as databases.
- **Code** – (written with a programming language)
- **Chromeless Browser** – a web browser that has the typical navigational elements removed so as to look like it is an app.
- **Device Features** – the internal technology available in different devices such as, camera.
- **Feature** – a distinctive attribute or aspect of something
- **Framework** - A collection of libraries
- **Integrated Development Environment (IDE)** – A SDK plus a graphical user interface see https://en.wikipedia.org/wiki/Integrated_development_environment. In this book we presume that an IDE comes with a simulator to visual and test your apps.
- **IAP conversion rate** - the percentage of users who complete an in-app purchase within a free app.
- **Localisation** – the process of making something local in character or restricting it to a particular place.
- **Mobile Computing** – is human–computer interaction in which a computer is expected to be transported during normal usage, which allows for transmission of data, voice and video. Mobile computing involves mobile communication, mobile hardware, and mobile software. Communication issues include ad hoc networks and infrastructure networks as well as communication properties, protocols, data formats and concrete technologies. Hardware includes mobile devices or device components. Mobile software deals with the characteristics

T. Salter, *Technological and Business Fundamentals for Mobile App Development*, https://doi.org/10.1007/978-3-031-13855-3

and requirements of mobile applications. See https://en.wikipedia.org/wiki/Mobile_computing

- **Non-Technical** – for this book means understanding about the 'business/Admin' side of app development. Examples, user Interface design, target markets
- **Push Notifications** – the ability to send information to end users cell/mobile devices
- **Programming Language** – Used to write code, a set of rules and syntax that you follow to make a program that can be complied and executed by a device.
- **Responsive Website** – a website that has been programmed in such a way as to change size and appearance to fit different screen sizes.
- **Software Development Kit (SDK)** – A collection of tools that enables you to write and compile the code see https://en.wikipedia.org/wiki/Software_development_kit
- **Target Market** – A target market is a group of customers within a business's serviceable available market at which a business aims its marketing efforts and resources. A target market is a subset of the total market for a product or service. See https://en.wikipedia.org/wiki/Target_market
- **Technical** – for this book means: Programming, programming design and architecture, programming languages, details about hardware such as, servers (type, security features etc.). Plus software such as, frameworks and internet protocols etc.
- **White Label App** – White Label is a term for using a template and then producing various different apps or websites from the initial template.

Bibliography

1. **Apps, The Business Of.** Stages of app development. [Online] https://www.businessofapps. com/insights/stages-of-app-development/.
2. **Wikipedia.** English Speakers. [Online] • https://en.wikipedia.org/wiki/ List_of_languages_by_number_of_native_speakers.
3. **Typedia.** Typedia Fonts. [Online] http://typedia.com/learn/only/typeface-classifications/.
4. **Awareness, Colour Blind.** [Online] https://www.Colourblindawareness.org.
5. **Organization, World Health.** World Health Organization Health Topics Coronavirus. *World Health Organization International.* [Online] https://www.who.int/health-topics/ coronavirus#tab=tab_1.
6. **Wikipedia.** Stay-at-home_order. [Online] https://en.wikipedia.org/wiki/Stay-at-home_order.
7. Office, UK Home. Coronavirus (COVID-19): Support for Victims of Domestic Abuse. [Online] 2020. https://www.gov.uk/government/publications/coronavirus-COVID-19-and-domestic-abuse/coronavirus-COVID-19-support-for-victims-of-domestic-abuse.
8. **BBC.** Coronavirus: Domestic Abuse Calls up 25% Since Lockdown, Charity Says. [Online] 2020. https://www.bbc.co.uk/news/uk-52157620.
9. *The pandemic paradox: The consequences of COVID-19 on domestic violence.* **Bradbury-Jones, C., & Isham, L.** s.l. : Journal of clinical nursing, https://doi.org/10.1111/jocn, 2020.
10. **WebMD.** The New Domestic Violence. *WebMD.* [Online] https://www.webmd.com/ mental-health/news/20201130/the-new-domestic-violence-technolog-abuse.
11. **Authority, The British Police.** Slient Solution Guide. [Online] https://www.policeconduct. gov.uk/sites/default/files/Documents/research-learning/Silent_solution_guide.pdf.
12. **Eaton, Adam.** British Broad Casting . *BBC.com.* [Online] https://www.bbc.com/news/ world-europe-56172456.
13. **Twitter.** Blog Twitter. [Online] https://blog.twitter.com/en_us/topics/product/2017/ introducing-twitter-lite.html.
14. **Wikipedia.** Tinder App. [Online] https://en.wikipedia.org/wiki/Tinder_(app)..
15. **Inc, Apple.** WWDC. [Online] https://developer.apple.com/wwdc21/.
16. **Wikipedia.** Reat Native. [Online] https://en.wikipedia.org/wiki/React_Native .
17. **Singer, P. W., & Friedman, A.** *Cybersecurity and cyberwar: What everyone needs to know.* s.l. : Oxford University Press, 2014.
18. **Guardian, The.** The Guardian Newspaper. [Online] https://www.theguardian.com/ technology/2021/apr/05/lg-to-pull-out-of-mobile-phone-market.
19. **Wikipedia.** Parler. [Online] https://en.wikipedia.org/wiki/Parler.
20. **Hill, The.** Tech Giants Crack Down on Parler. [Online] https://thehill.com/policy/ technology/533519-tech-giants-crack-down-on-parler-for-lack-of-content-mediation.

© The Editor(s) (if applicable) and The Author(s), under exclusive license to Springer Nature Switzerland AG 2022

T. Salter, *Technological and Business Fundamentals for Mobile App Development*, https://doi.org/10.1007/978-3-031-13855-3

21. **Insider, Apple.** Tim Cook looks to bring back Parler. [Online] https://appleinsider.com/articles/21/04/05/tim-cook-is-still-keen-to-bring-parler-back-to-the-app-store.
22. —. Parler. [Online] https://appleinsider.com/articles/21/04/05/tim-cook-is-still-keen-to-bring-parler-back-to-the-app-store.
23. **CNN.** Apple pulls I Am Rich. [Online] https://www.cnbc.com/id/26094329.
24. **CNBC.** [Online] https://www.cnbc.com/id/26094329.
25. **News, BBC.** Technology. [Online] https://www.bbc.com/news/technology-56713017.
26. **Inc, Apple.** App Store Review. [Online] https://developer.apple.com/app-store/review/.
27. **In, Apple.** App Store Review Guidelines. [Online] https://developer.apple.com/app-store/review/guidelines/.
28. **Standards, PCI Securtiy.** [Online] https://www.pcisecuritystandards.org/ .
29. **HHS.gov.** HIPAA. [Online] https://www.hhs.gov/hipaa/for-professionals/special-topics/health-apps/index.html .
30. **Annie, App.** [Online] https://www.appannie.com/en/ .
31. —. State-of-mobile-2021. *App Annie now known as Data.ai.* [Online] https://www.appannie.com/en/insights/market-data/state-of-mobile-2021/.
32. **Tamoco.** Ultimate App Montization Guide. [Online] https://www.tamoco.com/blog/ultimate-app-monetization-guide/ .
33. **Colony, Ad.** Mobile Monday. [Online] https://www.adcolony.com/blog/category/mobile-monday/. .
34. **Apps, The Buisness of.** [Online] https://www.businessofapps.com/data/app-revenues/.
35. **Tower, The Sensor.** [Online] https://sensortower.com/blog/sensor-tower-app-market-fore-cast-2025. .
36. **Deloitte.** [Online] https://www2.deloitte.com/us/en/insights/industry/technology/digital-media-trends-consumption-habits-survey/summary.html .
37. **Colony, Ad.** [Online] https://www.adcolony.com/blog/2021/09/05/mobile-monday-getting-creative-with-mobile-advertising-acceptable-ads-in-mobile-games-and-updated-app-reviews-on-android/.
38. **Google.** Banner Ads. [Online] https://support.google.com/google-ads/answer/7031480?hl=en.
39. —. Reward Ads. [Online] https://support.google.com/admob/answer/7372450?hl=en.
40. —. Admob. [Online] https://support.google.com/admob/answer/10159602.
41. **Statista.** [Online] https://www.statista.com/statistics/263797/number-of-applications-for-mobile-phones/ .
42. **Insider, Business.** [Online] https://www.businessinsider.com/the-app-race-to-the-bottom-is-real-2013-7. .
43. **Medium.** Skip Button. [Online] https://medium.com/swlh/how-much-money-do-youtubers-make-per-view-2390141a4922.
44. —. YouTubers. [Online] https://medium.com/swlh/how-much-money-do-youtubers-make-per-view-2390141a4922.
45. **Crunch, Tech.** [Online] https://techcrunch.com/2012/08/26/how-free-apps-can-make-more-money-than-paid-apps/?guccounter=1.
46. **Insider, Business.** Installs. [Online] https://www.businessinsider.com/just-2-of-app-installs-lead-to-purchases-2017-2?r=US&IR=T.
47. **MetaVerse.** Facebook company is now Meta. *About Facebook.* [Online] https://about.fb.com/news/2021/10/facebook-company-is-now-meta/.
48. **Wikipedia.** Angry Birds. [Online] https://en.wikipedia.org/wiki/Angry_Birds.
49. —. Rovio Entertainment. [Online] https://en.wikipedia.org/wiki/Rovio_Entertainment.
50. —. Angry Birds. [Online] https://en.wikipedia.org/wiki/Angry_Birds.
51. **Beat, Venture.** Angry Birds maker Rovio sets IPO price range that values company around $1 billion". [Online] venturebeat.com.
52. **TechCrunch.** Instagram seed funding. [Online] https://techcrunch.com/2010/03/05/burbn-funding/.
53. **Wikipedia.** Instagram. [Online] https://en.wikipedia.org/wiki/Instagram.

54. **Insider, Business.** [Online] https://www.businessinsider.com/facebooks-instagram-revenue-2013-10?r=US&IR=T.
55. **Wikipedia.** Twitter. [Online] https://en.wikipedia.org/wiki/Twitter .
56. **Quartz.** *Twitters IPO.* [Online] https://qz.com/145227/final-tally-twitters-ipo-was-bigger-than-googles-raising-2-1-billion/.
57. **TechCrunch.** The Birth Of Snapchat. [Online] https://techcrunch.com/2018/02/10/the-birth-of-snapchat/.
58. **Wikipedia.** Snapchat. [Online] https://en.wikipedia.org/wiki/Snapchat.
59. —. Snapchat. [Online] https://en.wikipedia.org/wiki/Snapchat.
60. **Journal, Wall Street.** Snap Chat Mulls Raising Money. [Online] https://www.wsj.com/articles/BL-DGB-30334.
61. **Quartz.** Snapchats inability to make money. *qz.com.* [Online] https://qz.com/97467/snapchats-complete-inability-to-make-money-is-the-reason-its-worth-800- million/ .
62. **Wikipedia.** Timeline of Snapchat. [Online] https://en.wikipedia.org/wiki/Timeline_of_Snapchat.
63. **Forbes.** Why is Snapchat Worth 20bn. [Online] https://www.forbes.com/sites/adamhartung/2016/05/27/why-is-snapchat-worth-20b-the-value-of-implementing-trends/#79392a453faa.
64. **Wikipedia.** Wordle. [Online] https://en.wikipedia.org/wiki/Wordle.
65. —. Agile Software Development. [Online] https://en.wikipedia.org/wiki/Agile_software_development.
66. **Scrum.** What is Scrum. [Online] https://www.scrum.org/resources/what-is-scrum.
67. **Hubspot.** [Online] https://www.hubspot.com/.
68. **SurveyMonkey.** [Online] https://www.surveymonkey.com/.
69. **Wikipedia.** Wordle. [Online] https://en.wikipedia.org/wiki/Wordle.
70. —. Instagram. [Online] https://en.wikipedia.org/wiki/Instagram .

Printed in the United States
by Baker & Taylor Publisher Services